Flavor Kitchen

Flavor Kitchen

Crystelle Pereira

Vibrant Recipes with Creative Twists

*Dedicated to my late grandad, Gregory De Souza,
who believed in me even before I did.*

Contents

Recipe Key

VE = Vegan
VG = Vegetarian
VeS = Vegan substitute
VgS = Vegetarian substitute

Introduction

The warmest welcome to my Flavor Kitchen! A habit of mine is to feed people the moment they set foot in the kitchen—and if they don't eat, I'll be very offended. So, my book is here to feed you at any time of day with flavor-packed dishes that are moreish, memorable and mouthwatering.

Anyone close to me, or who saw me on *The Great British Baking Show*, will know that I love my flavors. I cook and bake in the same way that I eat. If I go to a restaurant, I will never order a penne arrabiata, or a Victoria sponge. I always want to try something new; something exciting, interesting and unique. When I create my own dishes, it's exactly the same: I want to make something original.

So, I present to you a collection of my top 75 sweet and savory dishes, each with its own unique flavor combination that is balanced, powerful, and inspired by my travels, my heritage, or an unforgettable meal I have eaten. They're the sort of dishes that I hope will "wow" your dinner party guests, friends, family—or even yourself—with amazing taste sensations that you may have never experienced before.

Every single recipe in this book features flavors and ingredients that I genuinely love, and I am so excited to share them with you. Whether it's cardamom, gochujang, mango, cumin, yuzu, sesame, maple, or, of course, miso that features, I have absolutely loved developing—and eating—each and every dish, and I hope you love them just as much as I do.

I also want to assure you that this book is for cooks and bakers of all levels. I'm a family girl, so you'll find many sharing dishes designed to bring people together. But I also love a good party, so there are plenty of small plates and dips too! This book should have everything you're after: whether it's a curry, salad, or cake, there's a dish for every time of day, in every climate.

A BOOK OF TWO HALVES

This book is split into two halves—savory and sweet. Of course, I was fortunate enough to reach the final of *The Great British Baking Show*, so I had to share my favorite bakes, but I am equally passionate about cooking. Cooking was in fact my first love, starting from about age 6! Back then, my mom's nickname for me was "Chutney Mary" because, unlike my two elder sisters, I absolutely LOVED my food. I was the least fussy eater in the world (a parent's dream, I guess!) and enjoyed all the curries, samosas, spicy chutneys... just about everything. As well as being obsessed with eating, I was also drawn to the cooking process. I used to watch my mom in the kitchen (the same kitchen I use today), cooking away at the stove. She used to feed me bits of food on the side as she was cooking, which was mainly why I would stick so close, but I was also genuinely fascinated by cooking. Then, she started asking me to help her, and hired me as her Chief Taste Tester. She would ask me to taste her curries—not just eat, but taste. Could a savory dish be balanced with a pinch of sugar or jaggery, a sweet recipe be improved with a pinch of salt, or would adding lemon juice or vinegar cut through rich flavors for that all important "tang"? I had to close my eyes and really think about the flavor sensations in my mouth. Very often just the simplest addition would transform a dish and make it perfect. My mom is the one who not only instilled a love of food in me, but also who taught me the all-important foundations of flavor. She helped me develop my palate at such a young age, and that is really what got me into flavor-led cooking and baking.

MY FAVORITE FLAVORS

I count myself extremely fortunate to have traveled to so many different countries around the world, including Mexico, Japan, and South Korea. I also spent a year living in Spain and France as part of my Modern Languages degree. For me, food is by far the most important part of any culture. If I don't eat well on holiday, my trip is unsuccessful. I usually research the best, local cuisine in the place I'm traveling to (and we're not talking about fancy bars or rooftop restaurants—but rather tiny shacks with a queue of locals waiting outside) and then eat my way through the city. Also, I live in

London, which is bursting with incredible restaurants showcasing cuisines from around the world. I appreciate that I might be coming across as greedy, so I'll just have to hold my hands up and accept that.

From everything I've tasted, certain flavors or ingredients have really made an impression; for instance, trying yuzu for the first time in Hong Kong in a herbal tea, gochujang in South Korea, and when I had an incredible za'atar-topped hummus at a Lebanese restaurant in London. These experiences inspired me to search for those key ingredients and use them in my own cooking and baking.

There is also a good handful of dishes in this book that are rooted in my Portuguese-Goan heritage, or other areas across India. Goa was colonized by the Portuguese, and that has really influenced the cuisine, resulting in an eclectic mix of ingredients, such as vinegar, fresh green chiles, turmeric, coriander, coconut, and tamarind. I may be biased, but Goan food is my favorite cuisine in the world; I am a "Chutney Mary" after all.

You'll notice that with the Goan dishes, I've opted to keep a few of them traditional, as they're family recipes that have been passed down through generations—the key ingredients really shine through to provide the rich, tangy, and spicy flavors that are so iconic to the cuisine. In other dishes, however, I have put twists on classics, such as potato bhaji skins and a chai tres leches cake! These recipes are fundamentally fusions: taking the flavors and essence of a dish, and placing it in a different, but still familiar, setting. Thankfully, they all have my family's stamp of approval, which makes me very proud (because—trust me—they are often hard to please, especially Mum)!

I know many of us don't like the word fusion, but I prefer to think of it as a celebration of different cultures. I will never claim to be an expert in a cuisine whose culture I don't belong to, but I will say that I am a sucker for interesting and bold flavors, and I'm heavily influenced by the huge variety of cuisines I consume from around the world. So, you'll find that many recipes take the concept of a classic dish from one cuisine, but with flavors from a completely different one. For example, instead of standard sausage rolls, I've created hoisin duck "sausage" rolls. I've taken the familiar vessel of mac 'n' cheese, but added all the flavors and textures of a Greek spanakopita. I've got no standard flapjack recipe, but instead I have baklava-inspired flapjacks, full of nuts and a fragrant syrup. I am not by any means attempting to "improve" these classics but rather, I'm simply adding a "Crystelle twist"!

WHAT YOU'LL TAKE AWAY

My hope is that, as you cook and bake your way through this book, you will acquire a handful of new "pantry essentials" that you can turn to whenever you want to add a punch of flavor to your dishes. Ideally, you will all have a jar of miso in your refrigerator by the end of this book! As well as celebrating a host of new flavor combinations, I will also

reveal how to make the most out of your ingredients, with all my best tips and tricks, such as roasting nuts before you use them, mixing citrus peel with sugar, or frying off your spices.

For every "nonstandard" ingredient such as gochujang or ras el hanout, I have made sure that there are at least two recipes that use it. This means that you won't buy an ingredient for just one recipe and will see how versatile these ingredients are. All my favorite hero ingredients and flavors are explored in more detail in my Pantry Ingredients section on page 10.

The majority of the savory dishes are either vegetarian or vegan. I love meat, chicken, and seafood, but I also love the beauty of vegetables, legumes, and beans, and they can carry so much flavor when paired with the right ingredients. I have indicated whether a recipe is vegetarian (VG), vegan (VE), has a vegetarian substitute (VgS) or vegan substitute (VeS) available.

I've been told I like to waffle (no food pun intended) and it looks like that hasn't changed, but I'll stop my rambling here... All that's left to say here is happy cooking, happy baking, and enjoy the ride!

Lots of love & God bless,

Crystelle xxx

My Pantry Ingredients

Here you'll find a breakdown of all the "fun" ingredients that I use in my recipes—there may be things you have not used before, and others you are more familiar with. I've created this to give you the confidence to use every single ingredient that is called for in my book, because they are all accessible, versatile, and, most importantly, key to making your dishes pack a punch of flavor!

Garlic Powder

What? Sometimes called garlic granules, this is a powder made from dehydrated garlic, which is concentrated in flavor. **How?** I add garlic powder whenever I want a quick, garlicky flavor. It's great in dressings and marinades, sprinkled on roast potatoes, or added to a bread crumb topping. **Favorite Recipes:** Five Spice Roasted Cauliflower (p. 88), Spicy Korean-inspired Smashed Potatoes (p. 110).

Curry Leaves

What? Curry leaves come from the curry tree and are popular across South Asia. The flavor is distinctive and slightly aromatic, but with a herby feel to it (a bit like bay leaves, but much more pungent). I treat them as I do spices, frying them off in oil to release their wonderful flavors. **How?** They pair really well with cumin, mustard seeds, and turmeric, and can be added to Indian-style stir-fries. Alternatively, you can crisp up the leaves in oil and use them as a garnish. **Favorite Recipes:** Potato Bhaji Skins (p. 32), Dhokla-inspired Cornbread Muffins (p. 108).

Ras el Hanout

What? Ras el hanout is a fragrant spice blend from Tunisia, Algeria, and Morocco. The name means "head of the store" in Arabic, alluding to the best spices that the seller has to offer. Every blend varies, but it is typically a mixture of cinnamon, ginger, and coriander, with other spices. **How?** It's very aromatic, so I like to pair it with something sharp (such as vinegar) or sweet (such as honey or maple syrup). It's perfect to add to roast potatoes, marinades for chicken, or fish, as well as breads or other savory baked goods. **Favorite Recipes:** Spiced Squash & Puy Lentil Salad (p. 86), Cheesy Olive Spiced Scones (p. 102).

Chinese Five Spice

What? Prominent in Chinese cuisine, this aromatic spice blend is made with at least five spices: cinnamon, fennel, star anise, Szechuan peppercorns, and cloves, although blends vary. **How?** The flavors are potent, so I suggest adding it bit by bit until you have your desired flavor. The aromatics pair very well with umami flavors like soy and miso. It works in marinades for meat, chicken, or fish, but it's also a great addition to stir-fries, noodles, or even roasted veggies. **Favorite Recipes:** Char Siu Pulled Pork (p. 64), Salt & Pepper Halloumi Fries (p. 96).

Green Cardamom Pods

What? As you may know, cardamom is an aromatic spice native to South Asia—but I urge you to only buy whole, green cardamom pods and not the powdered stuff, which doesn't have nearly as much flavor! All my recipes call for green and not black cardamom, which has a slightly different flavor. I always suggest using whole pods, toasting them to release their flavors, then blitzing them to a fine powder. If you're using a spice grinder, you can blitz the shells (just make sure you get them really fine), but if you're using a pestle and mortar, then remove the shells and just grind the black seeds inside. **How?** Cardamom is used in both sweet and savory dishes. It can be used on its own but I also like to pair it with citrus or spices like ginger and cinnamon. You can add a sprinkle to your porridge, poached fruits, whipped cream—the options are endless! **Favorite Recipes:** Pistachio, White Chocolate, & Cardamom Millionaire Shortbread (p. 158), Mango & Cardamom Cheesecake (p. 170).

Gochugaru

What? Gochugaru is essentially a Korean version of chili powder that's more coarsely ground. It is what gives gochujang and kimchi their iconic, spicy flavor. **How?** It can be used in the same way as chili powder or chili flakes, added to your stir-fried rice or sprinkled on noodles, grilled cheese, or soups. **Favorite Recipes:** Grilled Kim-Cheese (p. 24), Gochujang Egg-fried Rice (p. 50).

Za'atar

What? Za'atar is a beautifully balanced, herby spice blend mostly identified with Middle Eastern and Mediterranean cuisine. It is a combination of herbs, sumac, and sesame seeds, giving it a great texture. **How?** Za'atar is very versatile, great for adding a fresh, aromatic flavor to rich dishes. It could be added to roasted vegetables, or sprinkled on flatbreads, salads, and eggs. **Favorite Recipe** Za'atar Potato Hash with Baked Eggs (p. 22), Cheesy Olive Spiced Scones (p. 102).

1 Garlic Powder
2 Curry Leaves
3 Ras el Hanout
4 Chinese Five Spice
5 Green Cardamom Pods
6 Gochugaru
7 Za'atar

1 Yuzu Juice
2 Pistachio Cream
3 Vanilla Bean Paste
4 Dulce de Leche
5 Sweetened Mango Pulp

Yuzu Juice

What? Yuzu is a very aromatic and tart citrus fruit, with a flavor profile somewhere between lemon, clementine, and grapefruit. It originated in China but now grows in Japan, Korea, and other countries too. I've never got my hands on the actual fruit, so I always use bottled yuzu juice, which works a treat in my dishes. Do not get this confused with Yuzu extract or flavoring, which are not the same and are extremely bitter. **How?** The great thing about yuzu juice is that it is very potent, so a little goes a long way. I find that the sharp flavors pair well with something sweet or rich like white chocolate or coconut. You could also use it in salad dressings, glazes to brush on fish, or even a sweet tea or refreshing lemonade! Treat it in the same way as concentrated lemon/lime juice. **Favorite Recipes:** Coconut & Yuzu Shortbread (p. 146), Yuzu & White Chocolate Mousse (p. 212).

Pistachio Cream

What? Pistachio cream—or *crema di pistacchio*—is the pistachio equivalent of hazelnut spread, and in my opinion is even better. It's vivid green and smooth, with that lovely, rich flavor of roasted pistachios and notes of white chocolate. Don't get this confused with the "healthier" pistachio butters, which are just blended pistachios. Pistachio cream is sweetened with sugar and completely smooth. You'll want to eat it by the spoonful. **How?** This can be used as you would hazelnut spreads: in buttercreams, swirled through cakes or cheesecakes, and even spread on toast. I love to add a heaping teaspoon of pistachio cream to my matcha lattes, as it pairs really well with the slightly bitter matcha. **Favorite Recipes:** Pistachio, White Chocolate, & Cardamom Millionaire Shortbread (p. 158), Pistachio, Orange, & Cardamom Carrot Cake (p. 180).

Vanilla Bean Paste

What? Vanilla bean paste is an amplified version of vanilla extract, and you'll only understand how much better it is once you try it in your baking. It's a thick paste, full of vanilla seed flecks. It is slightly more expensive than extract but, I promise you, it's really worth it. **How?** Use it where you want the vanilla flavor to stand out or complement other flavors. I think of vanilla as the sweet version of "seasoning". **Favorite Recipes:** Maple, Pecan, & Apple Popcorn Bites (p. 142), Tahini, Peanut, & White Chocolate Blondies (p. 165).

Dulce de Leche

What? Dulce de leche is a rich, sweet, caramel-like spread that originates in South America. It means "caramelized milk" in English, as it's made by slowly heating condensed milk for hours. **How?** My recipes call for condensed milk (widely available in grocery stores and online), that you submerge in a large pan of water and boil for a few hours, which turns it into dulce de leche. However, you can also buy premade dulce de leche. It is a good caramel sauce substitute, so it can be swirled into brownies, drizzled over ice cream or apple crumble or even sandwiched between cookies. Dulce de leche doesn't set like regular caramel, so would not work in recipes like millionaire shortbread. **Favorite Recipes:** Pecan, Coconut, & Caramel Brownies (p. 162), Tahini, Dulce de Leche, & Chocolate Chip Ice Cream (p. 210).

Sweetened Mango Pulp

What? Mango pulp is blitzed mango, sweetened with sugar syrup. It's smooth, sweet, and tastes almost like mango concentrate. **How?** Fresh mangoes are my favorite fruit but I almost always use sweetened mango pulp in my recipes. This is because mango pulp has a guaranteed sweet, concentrated flavor, and if your mangoes are slightly underripe, the flavor in your dishes just won't be as prominent. Mango pulp mixed with some milk and a pinch of cardamom makes the best mango milkshake too. **Favorite Recipes:** Mango & Cardamom Cheesecake (p. 170), Mango & Passionfruit Jelly Roll (p. 183).

Browned Butter

What? This isn't an ingredient per se, but a result of cooking down butter to completely change the flavor profile. You simply melt butter just past the point of melting, so that the milk solids brown and give off a lovely nutty aroma. This is why it is also known as *beurre noisette* (hazelnut butter). **How?** You can use brown butter in any recipe that calls for regular butter, but where you want a nuttier, richer flavor. Just be mindful that if you're browning butter, it loses moisture during the process so make sure you reweigh it afterward. **Favorite Recipes:** Miso Tahini Oat Cookies (p. 150), Pecan Pie Skillet Cookie (p. 154).

Stem Ginger

What? Stem ginger is the wonderfully sweet and spicy preserved young root of ginger. It comes stored in a syrup, and the ginger bulbs are firm yet slightly soft. The syrup should also not be overlooked, as it is laced with a punchy ginger flavor. **How?** It pairs well with richer flavors, such as chocolate and coconut. You could also stir stem ginger through caramel, cheesecakes, or ice cream. The syrup works perfectly in sweet sauces, and can also be used to flavor drinks or cocktails instead of simple syrup. **Favorite Recipes:** Ginger, Coconut, & Dark Chocolate Knobbly Oat Cookies (p. 156), Fig & Rose Mascarpone Cheesecake Bars (p. 190).

My Pantry Ingredients

Gochujang

What? Gochujang is a spicy, slightly sweet and aromatic fermented chili paste, originating in Korea. It also contains fermented soya beans, as well as several other ingredients, including red chile peppers. **How?** This definitely isn't something that should be eaten alone or as a dip, because the flavor is very strong and umami. It needs to be diluted or cooked out to release all of the flavors, or offset with something sweet or sharp. You can also use gochujang in a glaze to coat fried chicken or some fish, or even add a spoonful to a large broth or stir-fried noodles for some spice and a bit of umami. **Favorite Recipes** Korean-inspired Garlic Bread (p. 98), Spicy Korean-inspired Smashed Potatoes (p. 110).

Harissa Paste

What? Harissa is another fragrant chili paste, but originating in Tunisia and infused with spices like coriander, paprika, and cumin. **How?** Harissa is best paired with something sweet or rich, to balance out the spice. You could also mix it with mayonnaise to create a spiced dip, add it to salad dressings or to your grilled cheese. **Favorite Recipes:** Harissa Shrimp Spaghetti (p. 40), Slow-roasted Harissa Carrots (p. 92).

Miso Paste

What? Miso is a fermented soya bean paste that originated in Japan. It has a wonderful depth of rich, salty, and umami flavors that lifts almost any dish you add it to, whether sweet or savory. I like to call it salt on steroids. You get different types of miso, some richer than others, so if you're using it for the first time I recommend white miso, which is perfectly balanced. **How?** Miso is extremely versatile—I often use it in desserts to balance out sweet flavors but you can also mix it with something rich and creamy like butter or add it to marinades, salad dressings or glazes. **Favorite Recipes:** Miso Butter Mushroom Tagliatelle (p. 54), Miso, Peanut, & Date Banana Bread (p. 138).

Tamarind Concentrate

What? Tamarind is a sticky, sour fruit that comes from a legum nous tree, native to Africa, although it is prominent in Goan and Sri Lankan food. As the tamarind fruit is firm and sticky, the easiest way to use it is in the form of a paste or concentrate, that is thick, runny, and dark. There are different forms of tamarind paste—some lighter than others. The one I always use in my cooking is very rich and dark—t almost looks like treacle. This variety is strong in flavor so a little goes a long way. Don't get this confused with tamarind chutney, which is delicious but sweetened, mixed with other ingredients and used as a dipping sauce,

so not as strong as the concentrate. **How?** Tamarind is predominantly sour, so is often added to curries to cut through the richness. It can, however, be paired with sweet and salty flavors like honey and soy, and used to glaze chicken wings, for example. **Favorite Recipe:** Potato Bhaji Skins (p. 32), Goan Egg Caldine Curry (p. 66).

Tahini

What? I like to describe tahini as the sesame version of peanut butter. It's a paste made from ground sesame seeds, and is a Middle Eastern condiment. It's nutty, creamy, and rich. **How?** Tahini can be used in both sweet and savory dishes. It's most commonly known for its role in hummus, providing that iconic, nutty flavor, but it also works wonderfully in salad dressings to provide creaminess or as a spread in a wrap. In desserts, I love to pair the rich nuttiness with sweet, almost caramel-like flavors. You can also swirl tahini through banana bread or mix it with maple syrup to create a very mellow, nutty, caramel-y sauce. The options are endless! **Favorite Recipes:** Spiced Squash & Puy Lentil Salad (p. 86), Tahini, Peanut, & White Chocolate Blondies (p. 165).

Chipotle Paste

What? Chipotle paste is a fragrant Mexican chile paste, made from blitzed chipotle peppers, with a smoky and spicy flavor. **How?** I like to offset this with sweet and fresh flavors, such as like honey and lime. It also works beautifully in marinades for meat or fish, and you can even use it to flavor pastas, like mac 'n' cheese! **Favorite Recipes:** Honey & Chipotle-baked Camembert (p. 112), Chicken Burrito Fried Rice (p. 42).

Kimchi

What? Kimchi is a spicy and tangy fermented cabbage that is a staple side dish in Korean cuisine. **How?** It works as a refreshing accompaniment to rice, stirred through some stir-fried noodles, or paired with something a bit richer. Kimchi is delicious on its own, but, when cooked, you concentrate some of the flavors, and cook off some of the tanginess. **Favorite Recipes:** Grilled Kim-Cheese (p. 24), Gochujang Egg-fried Rice (p. 50).

Plum Sauce

What? Plum sauce is a thick, sticky, sweet, and slightly sour sauce that is often used in Cantonese and Chinese cooking. **How?** It's usually offset with saltier flavors, like soy or miso, and often aromatics, like ginger and garlic. It can be used in marinades, glazes, or dips, adding a sweet dimension. **Favorite Recipes:** Char Siu Pulled Pork (p. 64), Hoisin Duck "Sausage" Rolls (p. 104).

1 Gochujang
2 Harissa Paste
3 White Miso Paste
4 Tamarind Concentrate
5 Tahini
6 Red Miso Paste
7 Chipotle Paste

A Note on Vinegar

In any Goan recipe, the most traditional vinegar to use is coconut vinegar, which is made from the sap of coconut trees. It's dark and rich, with a similar flavor profile to malt vinegar (it doesn't taste of coconut). However, it is very hard to source, so all my Goan recipes either use apple cider vinegar or malt vinegar, both of which work well.

A Note on Oils

You'll notice that most of my recipes call for coconut oil for frying, as it has a high smoke point. You can absolutely replace this with another oil with a high smoke point, such as avocado oil. You want an oil with a high smoke point because when you fry things over high heat, the oil can burn and smoke if it can't withstand high heat. For recipes where things are being cooked over medium heat, I have used olive oil—but make sure this is regular olive oil, not extra virgin, which should be used uncooked in salad dressings or dips. In baked recipes, however, please don't substitute coconut with another oil. Coconut oil in baking adds a subtle sweetness so using a different oil like avocado or canola will alter the flavor completely.

A Note on Spices

Please make sure your spices are in date. Note that the older your spices, the less potent the flavors will be.

A Note on Milks

Some recipes call for full-fat coconut milk (sold in cans), which should not be confused with drinkable coconut milk (sold in cartons, and used as a dairy-free milk alternative to soya, almond, or oat milk). Aside from coconut milk, many of my recipes call for different types of "drinking milks," such as whole milk, almond milk or oat milk, as they each pair well with different flavors. You can, however, just use one type of milk for all these recipes and the properties should not differ greatly, but the flavor will not be the same.

A Note on Pastry

In any recipe that calls for puff pastry, we're using store-bought pastry. Yes, I'm a baker and love making puff pastry every now and then, but I also wanted these recipes to be as simple as possible, and I honestly believe that the prerolled puff pastry out there is perfect. With pie dough, all recipes call for homemade pastry as pie dough is much simpler and quicker to make. Also, all my pie dough recipes are infused with different spices and nuts. You can use shop-bought if you're short on time - you just won't get the added flavours from the homemade stuff.

A Note on Butter

All recipes call for unsalted butter—this is so that we can control the amount of salt in our dishes. I also always use a good quality butter in my dishes, which is very important for flavor and makes a particularly big difference in baking too. In some recipes—particularly when it comes to baking—the temperature of the butter plays an important role. For these recipes, I have specified when butter should be either cold or at room temperature. If the temperature of butter has not been specified, then either chilled or warm can be used.

A Note on Eggs

All eggs used in the recipes are extra large (which is large in the UK). These should all be at room temperature when used. If a recipe calls for egg whites or yolks only, remember that you can freeze both the yolks and whites in a freezer bag then defrost and use as normal at a later date to prevent any waste.

A Note on Onions

Many recipes call for brown onions—these are white on the inside with a brown skin on the outside. These are much more pungent than white onions, which are sweeter, milder, and often larger than brown onions. Where recipes ask you to brown your onions in a pan, make sure not to rush, as the browning process adds so much flavor.

A Note on Baking

For all baked recipes, remember that baking times will vary depending on your ovens, so please also look for visual signs in your baked goods are done to ensure that they are fully baked (such as a skewer coming out clean when inserted into a cake). Please make sure your yeast, baking powder and baking soda are all in date; I have had way too many baking disasters thanks to one of these ingredients being out of date! When it comes to yeast, simply add it to some warm liquid and wait for about 5 minutes. If the mixture does not froth up, then your yeast should be discarded.

This QR code will take you to more information on my hero ingredients, including my favorite brands and where you can buy them.

Sav

ory

Za'atar Potato Hash with Baked Eggs **22**

Grilled Kim-Cheese **24**

Goan Chicken Chili Fry **26**

Miso Salmon & Garlic Spinach Crêpes **28**

Potato Bhaji Skins **32**

Spicy Chorizo Baked Beans **34**

Goan-inspired Coconut & Cabbage Fritters **36**

Brunch & Lunch

Za'atar Potato Hash with Baked Eggs

I recently tried batata harra for the first time; a delicious, spicy Lebanese potato dish. Immediately, I thought to myself, "this would work so well in a potato hash" and, lo and behold, it worked a treat. To really capitalize on those Middle Eastern flavors, I've added fragrant za'atar to the potatoes (see Ingredients Pantry on page 10) and this, offset with the lemon, sherry vinegar, and freshness of the cilantro, really takes your tastebuds on a journey. This is perfect for brunch—warm, filling and comforting, and I hope that it becomes a staple for you!

2 large white potatoes, peeled and diced (1¾ cup diced)

3 tablespoons coconut or avocado oil

2 small red onions, diced

2 tablespoons sherry vinegar

1½ tablespoons za'atar

2 teaspoons garlic powder

1 teaspoon fine sea salt, plus extra for boiling

½ teaspoon ground black pepper

½ teaspoon chili flakes (or less if you don't want too much spice)

1 small bunch of cilantro, finely chopped

1 garlic clove, minced

juice of ½ lemon

2 extra-large eggs

1. Preheat the oven to 425°F/200°C fan/gas mark 7.

2. Add the diced potatoes to a large pan of cold, salted water. Bring this to a boil and cook the potatoes for 10 minutes, until they can be pierced with a knife but are still firm. Drain and set aside.

3. Place the oil in a large (10in) ovenproof skillet over medium heat. Once hot, add in the potato and onions and fry for a couple of minutes until the onions have softened and the potatoes are slightly browned. Then, add the sherry vinegar, za'atar, garlic powder, salt, pepper, and chili flakes and toss everything together until nicely coated.

4. Transfer the skillet to the oven and bake for 20 minutes, tossing everything halfway through, until the potatoes are slightly crispy around the edges and golden.

5. Sprinkle over the cilantro, garlic, and lemon juice and give everything a final mix. Then, make two wells in the mixture and crack an egg into each well.

6. Switch the oven to the broil setting and place the skillet under the broiler for about 5 minutes, until the eggs are cooked and the whites are completely opaque. Once cooked, I love to dip the potatoes into the runny yolk before devouring!

Grilled Kim-Cheese

When I'm working from home, a quick sandwich is always my go-to meal. But it has to pack a punch with flavor and texture and that's how I came up with my Grilled Kim-Cheese! Kimchi is a beautiful ingredient—fermented cabbage that is tangy, salty, and spicy, and, paired with some sharp cheese, cuts through the richness perfectly. To make this grilled cheese better than any other grilled cheese you've ever made, we're coating the bread in sesame seeds for that extra crunch and nutty flavor.

Kewpie mayo is a rich, sweet, and sharp Japanese mayo—so definitely use store-bought if you can get your hands on it. For those who can't, you can make my cheat's version at home with pantry ingredients.

2 slices of white crusty bread
  (e.g. sourdough)
2 tablespoons unsalted butter
2 heaping tablespoons kimchi
2 scallions, finely sliced with
  the white and green parts separated
3 tablespoons (¾oz) grated cheddar
2 tablespoons (½oz) grated mozzarella
2 tablespoons sesame seeds
½ teaspoon gochugaru or chili
  powder

for the kewpie mayo

2 tablespoons mayonnaise
½ teaspoon rice wine vinegar
¼ teaspoon superfine sugar
¼ teaspoon sesame oil

1. First make the kewpie mayo. Place all the ingredients in a small bowl and mix well to combine.

2. Spread 1 teaspoon of kewpie mayo on each slice of bread and set aside.

3. Melt 1 tablespoon of butter in a large skillet over low heat until warm. Add the kimchi and white parts of the scallions and fry for about 2–3 minutes until fragrant. Remove these from the pan and set aside, leaving all the juices in the pan.

4. Arrange the grated cheddar on one slice of bread over the mayo, then top with the cooked kimchi and white parts of the scallions, followed by the mozzarella. Sprinkle the green parts of the scallions over the mozzarella, then top with the second piece of the bread, mayo-side down, and press down firmly.

5. Spread 1 teaspoon of kewpie mayo over the top of the sandwich and sprinkle over 1 tablespoon of sesame seeds. Press these down into the bread; they should stick to the mayo.

6. Add 1 tablespoon of butter and ½ teaspoon gochugaru or chili powder to the skillet over medium–low heat and stir until combined and melted.

7. Place the sandwich in the pan, sesame-side down, and cook for 3–4 minutes. During this time, carefully spread the remaining mayo over the top of the sandwich, sprinkle with sesame seeds and press down.

8. After 3–4 minutes, carefully flip the sandwich, and fry for another 3–4 minutes, until the bread is toasted and golden, with a lovely crispy sesame seed crust.

9. Once cooked, carefully remove from the pan, slice in half and enjoy!

Goan Chicken Chili Fry

The zingy, fresh flavors of this chicken chili fry are true to my Portuguese-Goan heritage and it's also a family staple because it is such a simple dish to whip up with just a handful of ingredients. It's the perfect way to use up leftover roast chicken and you can either serve it on its own or in a wrap with some sweet chili sauce. And, you can absolutely choose whatever protein you like here—tofu works well, but also shrimp and beef—the world is your oyster.

2 medium white potatoes, peeled, halved, and sliced into ½in thick strips
3 tablespoons coconut oil, for frying
2 large brown onions, thinly sliced
½ teaspoon ground turmeric
2 thin green chiles/Indian finger chiles, sliced lengthwise down the middle
½ large cooked chicken (see Tips), shredded (I usually use leftovers from a roast)
5 tablespoons vinegar (malt vinegar or apple cider vinegar)
1 large bunch of fresh cilantro, finely chopped
fine sea salt and ground black pepper

1. Place the potato slices in a large pot of cold, salted water, cover the pan and bring to a boil. Once boiling, cook for 10 minutes (they should still be firm and hold their shape), then drain and set aside.

2. Melt 2 tablespoons coconut oil in a large skillet over medium heat. Add the onion slices, with a pinch of salt, and fry for 20–30 minutes until nicely browned. Please be patient with your onions, as browning them properly is key to adding so much flavor to your dish.

3. Using a slotted spoon, remove the onions and add 1 tablespoon of coconut oil to the pan. Turn the heat up to high and add the potatoes, tossing them in the oil to crisp up. Sprinkle over the turmeric and stir for about 7 minutes, until the potatoes take on a yellow hue and are crisp and golden around the edges.

4. Add the sliced chiles and shredded chicken to the pan with the potatoes and season well with salt and pepper. Stir to combine, frying for a couple of minutes.

5. Pour in the vinegar and return the onions to the pan, then stir for a minute to cook off the vinegar slightly.

6. Sprinkle over the cilantro and stir once more to combine before serving.

TIPS

You can also start with uncooked chicken—boneless, skinless chicken thighs, sliced into thin strips. Fry these in the hot pan (after removing the onions and potatoes) for 10–15 minutes, seasoning with salt and pepper and a sprinkle of turmeric. When cooked, return the veggies to the pan and continue with the remaining steps.

To make this vegan, simply swap the chicken for tofu, which I have done before and it tastes sublime! Just fry the tofu using the same method if using uncooked chicken, but for 1–2 minutes on each side.

Miso Salmon & Garlic Spinach Crêpes

I lived in Paris for six months and the one thing I couldn't get enough of was savory crêpes—or *galettes*, as they're called in France. These thin, soft pancakes, encasing a hot, rich filling, were such a comforting experience, full of contrasting flavors and textures. So here is my version, with the most "un-French" filling—miso-glazed flaked salmon with spinach and mushrooms, flavoured with garlic and sesame—but trust me, it's a dream. And I should also mention that these are somewhat special crêpes, with earthy olive oil, a hint of garlic powder and a bit of miso in the batter, which lend a lovely savoriness that pairs perfectly with the filling. The recipe looks long, but it's really just a combination of three simple recipes—the crêpes, spinach, and salmon.

for the crêpes

scant 1½ cups (11½fl oz) whole milk
1 teaspoon white miso paste
2 tablespoons (1fl oz) olive oil
1 extra-large egg
¼ teaspoon garlic powder
scant 1 cup (4oz) all-purpose flour
melted unsalted butter or coconut
   oil, for frying
pinch of fine sea salt and ground
   black pepper

for the miso salmon

2 tablespoons white miso paste
3 tablespoons rice wine vinegar
4 tablespoons
¼ teaspoon ground black pepper
1 teaspoon garlic powder
5 x 4oz salmon fillets
1 tablespoon coconut oil, for frying

for the spinach & mushrooms

1 tablespoon coconut oil
4 garlic cloves, finely chopped
3½ cup (7oz) shiitake mushrooms,
   sliced into strips
4½ cups (9oz) baby spinach
¼ teaspoon ground black pepper
2 teaspoons light soy sauce
1 teaspoon sesame oil
2 tablespoons sesame seeds

1. First, make the crêpes. Place 3 tablespoons of the milk in a small bowl and warm this in the microwave for 10–20 seconds. Add 1 teaspoon miso paste and whisk until it has dissolved, then transfer this mixture to a large bowl, along with the remaining milk, together with the olive oil, egg, garlic powder, salt, and pepper. Give this a good whisk until combined.

2. Place the flour in a large bowl and make a well in the center. Slowly pour in the wet mixture, whisking the batter constantly until completely smooth. Set this aside to rest while you marinate the fish and make the spinach.

3. In a large, deep dish, add 2 tablespoons miso paste, rice wine vinegar, 2 tablespoons maple syrup, black pepper, and garlic powder and whisk to combine and form a paste.

4. Toss the salmon fillets in the marinade until thoroughly coated, then cover and let marinate while you make the spinach.

5. Place the coconut oil in a large wok over medium heat, then fry the garlic for a minute, until fragrant and starting to turn golden. Add the mushrooms, turn the heat up to high, and fry them for 2–3 minutes, then add the spinach, black pepper, light soy sauce, and sesame oil and mix well to combine. Turn off the heat and continue stirring the spinach in the residual heat until just wilted. Immediately transfer the spinach and mushrooms to a separate dish (to prevent overcooking).

6. Wipe down the wok, making sure it is dry, then place over low heat and toast the sesame seeds for about 5 minutes, until golden. Sprinkle these over the spinach and mushroom mixture, tossing to combine.

7. Now you're ready to cook the crêpes. Using a brush, lightly grease a nonstick pan with melted butter or coconut oil, then place this over medium heat. Once warm, ladle a portion of pancake batter into the pan and quickly swirl this around until the batter has evenly coated the bottom. Fry for 2 minutes, until the edges start to pull away from the sides, then flip the crêpe carefully (using a spatula; flipping is optional) and cook for a couple of minutes.

Continued overleaf >>

"I like to think of miso as salt on steroids, and I have something of an obsession with it—the umami undertone it brings is unmatched. I used so much miso on *The Great British Baking Show* that it's become a part of my identity!"

8. Once cooked, I like to fold the crêpe in half, and then in half again and place this on a plate.

9. Repeat this process with the rest of the batter, until you have eight crêpes. Cover with some aluminum foil to stay warm while you fry the salmon.

10. Now fry the salmon. Heat the coconut oil in a large skillet over medium heat. Arrange the salmon fillets in the hot pan, skin-side down, and cook for 2 minutes. Flip the fillets and fry for another minute, until almost cooked.

11. Transfer the fillets to a plate, carefully peel off the skin and use two forks to gently break the flesh into large flakes. Pour the marinade from the dish into the pan and simmer over high heat for 20 seconds until slightly thickened. Stir through the flaked salmon and cook this for about 1 minute, until just cooked. Add the remaining maple syrup and stir to combine, then take off the heat.

12. Now assemble: Lay out a crêpe, add a spoonful of the spinach and mushroom mixture in the middle, leaving a 2in border. Sprinkle the miso salmon on top of the spinach, fold the top and bottom of the crêpe over the filling, then fold the two sides over to form a square, exposing some of the filling in the middle. (Alternatively, you can lay the fillings down the middle of the crêpe and simply roll up.)

TIPS

You can also serve the salmon and spinach with some sticky rice, as quicker alternative to crêpes.

Swap the salmon for some crumbled, firm tofu to make this dish vegetarian.

Potato Bhaji Skins

I made potato bhaji as one of my pastry terrine fillings during *The Great British Baking Show*, along with Lily Nana's Pickle Chicken Curry on page 72, which got me the coveted Hollywood Handshake—so you're in for a treat! It's a dry curry, with hardly any liquid content, and I love that it's got so many different flavors and textures. Here, by serving the bhaji in double-roasted potato skins, we add an extra layer of crunch, which pairs perfectly with the cooling cilantro yogurt dressing. Plus, it transforms a traditional curry into party food, which you can pick up with your hands and devour—perfect for games night, family get-togethers or pretty much any occasion. Finally—you'll never believe that this dish is 100 percent vegan!

for the roasted potatoes

7 tablespoons olive oil
1 teaspoon fine sea salt
½ teaspoon black pepper
¼ teaspoon ground turmeric
4 large baking potatoes, sliced
    in half lengthwise

for the potato bhaji

2 tablespoons coconut oil
4 teaspoons black mustard seeds
40 fresh curry leaves
3 teaspoons cumin seeds
4 small brown onions, finely diced
1in piece of fresh ginger, grated
6 garlic cloves, grated
½ teaspoon ground turmeric
4 teaspoons superfine sugar
6 tablespoons red-skinned peanuts
a small handful of cilantro, finely
    chopped
fine sea salt, to taste

for the cilantro yogurt dressing

a large handful of cilantro
1 green chili
1 garlic clove
½ cup (4¼oz) coconut yogurt
Juice of ½ lime
¼ teaspoon fine sea salt
½ teaspoon tamarind concentrate

1. Preheat the oven to 400°F/180°C fan/gas mark 6.

2. In a small bowl, mix 7 tablespoons of olive oil with the salt, pepper, and turmeric. Brush the potatoes with half this oil, and then place them, flesh-side down, in a large roasting pan, and transfer to the oven for 40 minutes, until soft and golden.

3. While the potatoes are roasting, make the bhaji. Place 1 tablespoon coconut oil in a large skillet over low heat and heat gently until melted, then fry the mustard seeds, curry leaves, and cumin seeds for a couple of minutes until fragrant, taking care not to burn.

4. Add the onions to the pan and fry for 20–30 minutes, until browned, then grate in the ginger and garlic, stir through the turmeric, and fry for 2 minutes until fragrant.

5. Take the roasted potatoes, and, on the flat side, use a knife to score a crosshatch in the flesh (making sure not to cut all the way through), then use a metal spoon to scoop out the potato, leaving a thin border of potato in the skins.

6. Brush the insides of the potato skins with the remaining turmeric oil, then return them to the oven and bake, skin-side down, for 20 minutes until crispy.

7. Add the diced potato flesh to the onion mix and stir to combine. Fry for 3 minutes, until the potatoes are coated in all of the spices, then season well with salt and sugar to taste. Add a splash of water to loosen slightly if necessary (a few tablespoons should be enough).

8. In a separate pan, warm the remaining coconut oil over high heat and fry the peanuts for about 4 minutes, until slightly browned. Once cooked, stir the peanuts through the bhaji mix along with the chopped cilantro, and take off the heat but keep warm.

9. Finally, make the cilantro dressing. Place all the ingredients in a food processor and blitz until smooth.

10. To assemble, fill the crispy potato skins with large spoonfuls of the potato bhaji. Drizzle over the cilantro dressing, then serve the remaining dressing in a small dish on the side.

Spicy Chorizo Baked Beans

Now, I'm not a fussy eater at all, but baked beans were something I just never really enjoyed. So, I started a quest to make them great, and with a handful of ingredients, this was so easy to do. Using humble canned cannellini beans and pureed tomatoes as the base, with the addition of rich, salty soy sauce, some maple syrup for sweetness, and tangy notes from red wine vinegar, you can create a beautiful balance of flavors. The star of the show, however, is the chorizo. By frying this off first, it releases all the spicy, smoky oils, which then flavor the rest of the dish. This is one of my favorite brunch dishes—I love it on some toast, or with eggs on the side.

1 tablespoon olive oil, for frying
¾ cup (4½oz) diced chorizo sausage
1 large red onion, finely diced
5 garlic cloves, finely chopped
½ teaspoon cayenne pepper
½ teaspoon chili flakes
1 x 14oz can cannellini beans, drained
1 cup (7oz) pureed canned tomatoes
1 tablespoon red wine vinegar
2 teaspoons light soy sauce
2 teaspoons maple syrup
½ teaspoon fine sea salt

1. Heat the oil in a large skillet over low heat and fry the chorizo for about 7 minutes, turning up the heat halfway, until the colorful, fragrant oils are released and the chorizo is slightly crispy around the edges. Using a slotted spoon, transfer the chorizo to a small dish, leaving the oils in the pan.

2. Add the red onion to the chorizo oils in the pan and fry over low heat for about 5 minutes until softened.

3. Add the garlic, cayenne pepper, and chili flakes and fry for another 2 minutes until fragrant.

4. Add the drained cannellini beans to the pan and stir gently for a couple of minutes until the beans are coated well in the oils then add the pureed tomatoes, red wine vinegar, soy sauce, maple syrup and salt and stir well to combine.

5. Simmer for a few minutes, until slightly thickened, then add back in the cooked chorizo and stir this through the beans. Serve and tuck in!

Goan-inspired Coconut & Cabbage Fritters

My mum makes this incredible stir-fried cabbage to accompany our curries; flavored with cumin, mustard seeds, a hint of turmeric and shredded coconut, which adds a slight sweetness. So one day, I thought—I wonder how this would work as a fritter? And I am pleased to report that the result is an absolute delight. I fry them in coconut oil to form crispy, aromatic patties and serve them with a cooling coconut yogurt dip, and every bite reminds me of home. I love them for brunch, with poached eggs on top.

1 large white potato (7–8oz), coarsely grated
1 medium brown onion, grated
1½ teaspoons fine sea salt
5 tablespoons coconut oil
7 curry leaves
2 teaspoons cumin seeds
1 teaspoon mustard seeds
¼ white cabbage (4½oz), finely shredded on a mandoline (about 1½ cups)
¼ cup (¾oz) shredded coconut
2 extra-large eggs
¼ teaspoon ground turmeric
2 tablespoons all-purpose flour
1 teaspoon ground black pepper
1 thin green chili/Indian Finger chili, finely diced

for the coconut yogurt dip

4 heaping tablespoons unsweetened coconut yogurt
juice of 1 lime
½ teaspoon garlic powder
a pinch of fine sea salt
¼ teaspoon chili powder

1. Place the grated potato and onion in a bowl with ½ teaspoon salt and mix well to combine. Transfer the mixture to a large colander over a sink and allow the excess moisture to drain while you prepare the rest of the ingredients.

2. Now temper the spices. Gently heat 1 tablespoon coconut oil in a skillet over low heat and, once warm, add the curry leaves, cumin seeds and mustard seeds, frying for a few minutes until fragrant, making sure not to burn them as they will turn bitter. Tip these spices into a large bowl.

3. Using your hands, squeeze out as much moisture as possible from the grated potato and onion then tip the drained mixture into the bowl with the spices, mixing well to combine. Add the cabbage, coconut, eggs, turmeric, flour, 1 teaspoon salt, pepper, and diced chili and give this one last final mix to combine everything together.

4. Now fry the fritters. Place the remaining oil in the same skillet used to temper the spices, over medium heat. Once the oil is hot, spoon a heaping tablespoon of the mixture into the hot oil, flattening it with the back of the spoon to make a fritter. Fry this for 2½ minutes on each side until crispy and golden, then transfer to a plate lined with paper towels, to soak up the excess oil. Repeat with the remaining batter.

5. Finally, make the dip. Place all the ingredients in a bowl and mix well to combine. To serve, dip the fritters in the yogurt sauce and enjoy!

Pasta, Rice, & Noodles

Harissa Shrimp Spaghetti

In my humble opinion, this pasta has it all. Harissa provides a lovely, earthy spiciness which is offset beautifully by a carbonara-style creaminess (egg yolks and Parmesan). With a bit of fresh lime to cut through the richness, a crispy bread crumb topping for that all-important texture, and juicy, flash-fried shrimp, this dish will really make your tastebuds sing.

for the bread crumbs

1 cup (2oz) bread crumbs
¼ cup (¾oz) grated Parmesan
1½ teaspoons garlic powder
½ teaspoon ground black pepper
1 teaspoon dried basil
3 tablespoons olive oil
1 teaspoon harissa paste

for the shrimp

9oz jumbo shrimp, uncooked, peeled and deveined
1 tablespoon olive oil
a good pinch of fine sea salt and ground black pepper

for the pasta sauce

9oz spaghetti
¾ cup (2¼oz) grated Parmesan
3 egg yolks
2 tablespoons olive oil
5 garlic cloves, finely diced/grated
2 tablespoons harissa paste
zest of ½ lime
juice of ½ lime
¼ teaspoon ground black pepper

TIP

I have also tried this spaghetti with flaked salmon and that works really well too, but you can also omit the shrimp to make this vegetarian.

1. First make the bread crumbs. Place all the ingredients except the oil and harissa paste in a large bowl and combine. Heat the oil in a large skillet over medium heat and stir through the harissa paste for about 30 seconds, until sizzling. Add the bread crumb mixture and cook, stirring, for 4–5 minutes, until the bread crumbs have taken on a light red color and become crispy. Remove from the heat, transfer to a bowl and set aside.

2. Now cook the shrimp in the same pan. Heat 1 tablespoon oil over medium-high heat, then fry the shrimp, seasoning with salt and pepper, for 2 minutes on each side, until opaque and pink. Using a slotted spoon, transfer them to a plate but leave the juices in the pan.

3. Now get your pasta boiling. Bring a large pot of heavily salted water to a boil and cook your spaghetti until just before al dente (so about 3 minutes less than the package directions). Reserve about 1 cup (8fl oz) of the starchy cooking water and set aside.

4. While the spaghetti is cooking, place the Parmesan and egg yolks in a bowl and whisk to form a thick paste. Add 5 tablespoons of the hot pasta water, 1 tablespoon at a time, whisking constantly until it forms a smooth liquid.

5. Heat the oil in the skillet used to cook the shrimp, and fry the garlic over low heat until fragrant, about 2 minutes. Stir through the harissa paste and fry this for another 5 minutes.

6. Add ½ cup (4fl oz) pasta water to the pan and mix with the harissa mixture. Then, using tongs, transfer the spaghetti noodles from the water straight into the pan. Give them a really good toss until fully coated in the harissa mixture, adding more cooking water as needed, until the noodles have absorbed the liquid and are fully cooked.

7. Take off the heat and pour in the egg yolk mixture. Using tongs again, toss the noodles until everything has combined, and the sauce looks creamy and glossy, adding more cooking water to loosen if needed.

8. Finally, stir through the lime zest and juice and season with pepper.

9. Serve with bread crumbs on top and enjoy immediately.

Chicken Burrito Fried Rice

I absolutely love burritos because the combination of rice, meat, and beans with some fresh salsa is just so perfectly balanced. Here, I take the essence of a burrito and turn it into a quick fried rice with crunchy tortilla chips and greens thrown in at the end for a fantastic texture. The guacamole and salsa are optional but highly recommended—they really take the dish to the next level. These are both a little tangier than your standard salsa and guac, with high quantities of lime juice to really cut through the richness of the fried rice.

for the chipotle chicken & veggies

2 tablespoons olive oil, for frying
1 medium brown onion, finely diced
3 teaspoons paprika
1 teaspoon cayenne
6 teaspoons chipotle paste
6 garlic cloves, finely chopped
1lb 5oz boneless chicken thighs, diced
1 red bell pepper, diced
1 x 14oz can black beans, drained
scant 1 cup (5oz) canned corn
1½ teaspoons fine sea salt
20 pickled jalapeño slices

for the lime & cilantro rice

3½ cups (1lb 5oz) cold precooked
    long grain rice
zest of 2 limes
juice of 1½ limes
a large handful of cilantro, finely
    chopped

for the salsa

1 red onion, diced
juice of 1 lime
2 small salad tomatoes, diced
a bunch of fresh cilantro, finely
    chopped
a pinch of fine sea salt and ground
    black pepper

Continued overleaf >>

1. Heat the oil in a large pan or wok over medium heat and fry the onion for about 10 minutes until softened and slightly browned. Add the paprika, cayenne, chipotle paste and garlic and fry for a few minutes until fragrant.

2. Add the chicken and cook until browned and well coated in the spices, for about 10 minutes, then add the red bell pepper and cook for another 2 minutes. Stir through the beans, corn, and salt, then taste and adjust the spices and seasonings as needed. Turn off the heat and set aside.

3. Take your cold rice and stir the lime zest and juice and cilantro through the rice with a fork, mixing well.

4. Turn the heat back on under your pan, add the rice mixture to the cooked chicken and veggies, and stir gently to combine for 2–3 minutes until hot, making sure not the break the rice. Finally sprinkle over the pickled jalapeños, then turn off the heat.

5. To make the salsa, place the red onion in a small bowl and cover with lime juice. Scrunch them with your hands to help the onions pickle faster, then add the tomato and cilantro and season with a pinch of salt and pepper.

Continued overleaf >>

for the guacamole

1 red onion, diced

juice of 2 limes

2 large avocados, halved, pitted, and
   the flesh scooped into a bowl

4 garlic cloves, finely chopped

1 bunch of fresh cilantro, finely
   chopped

1 green jalapeño, finely diced (optional)

fine sea salt and ground black pepper

for the garnish

1 small head Gem lettuce, thinly sliced

a handful of tortillas, crushed

2 large handfuls of grated mozzarella
   (optional)

TIPS

Swap the chicken for firm tofu, and
omit the cheese to make this vegan!

Don't use basmati rice here as it is
likely to break. Day old, cold rice is
perfect for this as it is less likely to
overcook.

As with any fried rice, the trick is to
have everything ready and prepared,
because the cooking process is
really quick and you don't want
anything to overcook.

6. Now make a quick guacamole. Place the red onion in a bowl,
   cover with the juice of 1 of the limes and, as before, scrunch
   the onion with your hands to help it pickle faster. Mash the
   avocados with a fork until almost smooth, then stir through
   the garlic and juice of the other lime. Mix through the cilantro
   and jalapeño and then add the pickled red onion and the
   juices. Finish with a good pinch of salt and pepper and give it
   all one last mix.

7. To serve, mix the greens through the fried rice, then spoon
   onto plates. Sprinkle crushed tortilla chips over the top, with
   the salsa and guacamole on the side. Finally, top with grated
   mozzarella if desired.

Vegan Miso Ramen

This is a vegan one-pot wonder—you dump everything in a pot and let it simmer away while you watch an episode of *Desperate Housewives*. So it's not a traditional ramen by any means. The longer you cook it for, the more intense the flavor—I've suggested a minimum of 1 hour, but you can leave it for a good few hours. Just remember to add the fresh vegetables and noodles after you've finished cooking the soup base, to avoid them going soggy. The only extra bit of cooking is flash-frying the mushrooms and pak choi, just to get a bit of color on them, which really enhances their flavor.

for the soup base

3.5 liters water
2 vegetable stock cubes
3 small brown onions, finely diced
1in piece of fresh ginger, cut into
    4 thick slices
5 garlic cloves, smashed
2 star anise
2 tablespoons white or red miso paste
1 teaspoon ground black pepper
½oz dried ceps (about 15)

for the soup add-ins

1 teaspoon coconut or avocado oil,
    for frying
2 cups (4¼oz) fresh shiitake
    mushrooms, sliced
2 heads of pak choi, leaves separated
    and stems sliced into strips
3 tablespoons light soy sauce
1 tablespoon dark soy sauce
2 tablespoons sesame oil
1 tablespoon rice wine vinegar
¼ teaspoon fine sea salt
2 tablespoons maple syrup
4 x 1¾oz nests of ramen noodles
fine sea salt and ground black pepper

for the garnish

1 block silken tofu (or protein of
    choice), cut into bite-size slices
5 scallions, finely sliced
sesame seeds
sesame oil
crispy chili oil

1. First make the soup base. Put the water and stock cubes in a large pot, and bring to a boil. Add all the remaining ingredients for the soup base except the ceps, mix well, and simmer for 45 minutes.

2. Place the dried ceps in a small bowl and cover with 2 cups (17fl oz) boiling water. Set aside to soak for about 10 minutes, then remove the mushrooms and cut them into small chunks using scissors. Add these to the soup, then add the mushroom liquid too, discarding any residue at the bottom of the bowl. Continue to simmer for at least another 15 minutes, or longer.

3. While the soup is cooking, heat the oil in a large skillet over high heat. Once hot, fry the fresh mushrooms for about 2 minutes and season with a pinch of salt and pepper. Then, add the pak choi stems and toss with the mushrooms for 30 seconds. Take off the heat and set aside.

4. After the broth has been cooking for 1 hour, add the seasonings: light soy sauce, dark soy sauce, sesame oil, rice wine vinegar, salt, and maple syrup. Mix well to combine.

5. Cook the ramen noodles directly in the soup for 5–7 minutes (or as long as the package says) until fully cooked, then take the pot off the heat.

6. To serve, use tongs to transfer the noodles to large serving bowls. Ladle over the soup (discarding the slices of ginger and star anise pods), and then garnish with the cooked mushrooms and pak choi stems, raw pak choi leaves, silken tofu, scallions, sesame seeds, and a drizzle of sesame oil and crispy chili oil, if you wish.

TIP

Tofu and veggie broth keep this completely vegan, but if you're not vegan, you can use beef broth and any protein of your choice, and you can also add any leftover meat or chicken bones to the soup base and boil these with the rest of the ingredients. Also, don't be alarmed by the quantities of soup you produce—don't forget that ramen is served in large bowls with ladles upon ladles of soup. Slurp away!

Spanakopita-inspired Mac 'n' Cheese

Mac 'n' cheese has got to be one of my favorite comfort foods of all time—I usually love to bake it with a really crispy bread crumb topping to encase that warm, gooey, and bubbling filling. So one day, I thought—what if we could make that bread crumb topping even crispier, and use phyllo pastry instead? And for me, phyllo pastry goes hand in hand with spanakopita—those crispy, aromatic pastry packages encasing a beautifully flavored spinach and feta filling. So, I've combined the two. And it works! I've also added some chopped artichokes, which is not conventional by any means. In my opinion, however, their nuttiness and slightly meaty texture pair beautifully with the spinach and feta, but feel free to leave them out—it's up to you!

for the spinach

1 tablespoon oil from the artichoke jar (or olive oil if not using artichokes)
5 garlic cloves, finely chopped
3½ cups (7oz) baby spinach
pinch of fine sea salt and ground black pepper
¼ cup (½oz) fresh dill
½ teaspoon dried oregano
6–8 canned, precooked artichokes (optional), diced

for the bechamel

1 tablespoon oil from the artichoke jar (or olive oil if not using artichokes)
3½ tablespoons (1¾oz) unsalted butter
5 garlic cloves, finely chopped
2 tablespoons all-purpose flour
2¼ cups (18fl oz) whole milk
2 bay leaves
1½ teaspoons ground black pepper
1 teaspoon fine sea salt
1 teaspoon mustard
¼ teaspoon ground nutmeg
2¼ cups (9oz) grated mozzarella
⅔ cup (2½oz) grated cheddar

for the macaroni

2¾ cups (9½oz) uncooked macaroni
7oz feta
7–10 sheets of phyllo pastry
1 tablespoon sesame seeds
extra oil for brushing the phyllo pastry

1. Preheat the oven to 400°F/180°C fan/gas mark 6.

2. First, prepare the spinach. Warm the oil in a large skillet over medium heat. Add the garlic and fry for 3–5 minutes until fragrant, then add the spinach and a pinch of salt and pepper, and cook for about 30 seconds until just wilted. When cooked, transfer to a large mesh strainer and place over the sink to allow the juices to strain.

3. Now make the bechamel sauce. Place the oil and butter in a large pan and melt over low heat. Add the garlic and fry for 3-5 minutes until fragrant. Stir through the flour and cook until slightly browned. Slowly pour in the milk, whisking constantly until smooth. Add the bay leaves, salt, pepper, mustard, and nutmeg, then cook over low–medium heat for 10–15 minutes, stirring constantly, until thickened. Once thickened, remove from the heat and stir through the cheddar and half the mozzarella.

4. Bring a large pot of heavily salted water to a boil and cook your macaroni until just before al dente (so about 3 minutes less than the package directions).

5. Remove the bay leaves from the bechamel. Add the cooked and drained macaroni to the bechamel, and stir to combine.

6. Squeeze as much water from the spinach as possible. Transfer it to a cutting board and finely chop along with the dill and oregano. Add the diced artichokes and mix to combine. Stir the mixture through the macaroni, stirring really well to combine. Finally, crumble in the feta and stir to combine.

7. Transfer half of the macaroni mixture to a deep, 5-quart Dutch oven and flatten it out. Sprinkle over the remaining mozzarella, then top with the remaining macaroni and flatten it out.

8. Brush one sheet of phyllo liberally with artichoke (or olive) oil. Scrunch this into a rough ball, and it on top of the macaroni. Continue doing this with the remaining phyllo sheets until the macaroni is fully covered. Sprinkle with sesame seeds.

9. Bake for 25 minutes, until the phyllo is golden and crispy. Serve warm and enjoy!

Gochujang Egg-fried Rice

I had to share this recipe because we make it once a week in our house. I like to think of it as egg-fried rice on steroids! The Korean red chili paste, gochujang, is the star of the show here (see Pantry Ingredients on page 10)—just a few tablespoons transforms the fried rice into a flavor sensation.

2 tablespoons coconut oil, for frying

4 extra-large eggs

½ teaspoon fine sea salt, plus an extra pinch

½ teaspoon ground black pepper, plus an extra pinch

2 tablespoons light soy sauce, plus an extra dash

5 scallions, finely sliced (white and green parts separated)

1in piece of fresh ginger, grated

8 garlic cloves, finely chopped

4 tablespoons gochujang

1 large carrot, peeled and finely diced

1 zucchini, finely diced

a small handful of kimchi, finely diced (optional)

4 cups (7½oz) shiitake mushrooms, finely diced

scant 1 cup (4½oz) frozen peas

3 tablespoons rice wine vinegar,

3 tablespoons sesame oil

½ teaspoon chili flakes or gochugaru

5 cups (1lb 12oz) cold precooked white rice (long or short grain)

juice of ½ lime

1. In a large wok, melt 1 tablespoon coconut oil over medium heat. In a bowl, whisk the eggs with salt, pepper, and a dash of soy sauce, then add to the pan and scramble until fully cooked, about a minute. Transfer to a plate and set aside.

2. Heat another tablespoon of oil in the wok and fry the white scallion parts with the ginger and garlic for 2 minutes until fragrant. Add the gochujang and fry this off for another 2 minutes.

3. Add the carrot and cook for a minute, then the zucchini, kimchi, and mushrooms and cook for 2 minutes. Add the frozen peas and mix these until thawed, about 2 minutes.

4. Add 2 tablespoons each of soy sauce, rice wine vinegar and sesame oil, along with the chili flakes and ½ teaspoon each of salt and pepper. Mix well to combine and cook for 2 minutes to allow it to thicken slightly.

5. Tip in the rice and use a large rubber spatula to mix everything well. Turn off the heat and add back in the cooked egg, along with the green parts of the scallion. Mix again.

6. Finally stir through the lime juice with the remaining rice wine vinegar and sesame oil.

TIPS

As with any stir-fry, make sure you have everything chopped and ready to go.

Another very important tip is to use cold rice. Leftover rice works best but, if you are making it fresh, allow it to cool down as much as possible. And finally, do not use basmati rice as it is prone to breaking—use long grain or short grain rice.

Remove the egg or replace it with tofu to make the recipe vegan.

'Nduja, Kale, & Mascarpone Rigatoni

I first made this pasta as a raid-the-refrigerator dinner, as we had some leftover kale and mascarpone in the refrigerator. I vividly remember creating this dish, because it really captured the essence of how I cook: I tasted and tasted, adjusting as I went along, until I ended up with a dish full of fun textures (crispy roasted kale), but also rich flavors (spicy 'nduja and creamy mascarpone), and all balanced out with the freshness of the lemon. If you're new to 'nduja, you're in for a treat. It's a spicy, spreadable Italian sausage that essentially melts as soon as it hits a hot pan, and creates the most warming and smoky flavor base to this dish.

for the crispy kale

5oz kale greens
2 tablespoons olive oil
1 teaspoon garlic powder
½ teaspoon fine sea salt
½ teaspoon ground black pepper

for the pasta

3 cups (9oz) rigatoni
3oz 'nduja
3 garlic cloves, finely chopped
4 heaping tablespoons mascarpone
zest of ½ lemon
juice of ¼ lemon
¼ cup (¾oz) grated Parmesan, plus
    extra to garnish
ground black pepper, to taste

1. Preheat the oven to 350°F/160°C fan/gas mark 4.

2. Rip your kale into bite-size pieces, removing any thick stems, and place on a large roasting pan. Toss with the olive oil, garlic powder, and salt and pepper and use your hands to ensure the leaves are well coated. Bake in the oven for 25 minutes until crispy, rotating the pan halfway through, then set aside.

3. Bring a large pot of heavily salted water to a boil and cook your rigatoni until just before al dente (so about 3 minutes less than the package directions). Reserve about 1 cup (8fl oz) of the starchy pasta water.

4. While the pasta is cooking, place a large skillet over medium–low heat and fry the 'nduja for a couple of minutes until it has turned into a sizzling, more liquid paste. Add the olive oil and garlic and fry over very low heat for 5 minutes until fragrant.

5. Add ½ cup (4fl oz) of the starchy pasta water to the pan and swirl to loosen the 'nduja a little, then stir through the mascarpone, mixing well to combine.

6. Then, using a slotted spoon, transfer the rigatoni from the water straight into the skillet. Give the pasta a really good toss until fully coated in the sauce. Add the lemon zest and juice, the Parmesan, and a little more pasta water as needed, to loosen the sauce, mixing well until glossy.

7. Take the pan off the heat, season with black pepper and stir through half the crispy kale. Toss together well, then serve sprinkled with the remaining kale and more parmesan, if you like.

TIP

Rigatoni is such a great pasta—those huge tubes are so impressive—but of course you can use whatever you have in your cupboard. Just try and find something with ridges, to really hold all of that lovely creamy sauce.

Pasta, Rice, & Noodles

Miso Butter Mushroom Tagliatelle

This is one of my prized vegetarian recipes because it is ridiculously simple and packed full of flavor. I like to think of miso as an alternative to Parmesan—it acts like a seasoning, with that unbeatable umami flavor—and, in this recipe, it pairs beautifully with butter to form a creamy, savory, and rich pasta sauce. And please, don't ignore that squeeze of lemon juice at the end—it cuts through the richness perfectly and completely lifts the entire dish.

3 tablespoons (1½oz) unsalted butter
2½ cups (5¼oz) mushrooms (chestnut or shiitake), thickly sliced
7oz tagliatelle
5 garlic cloves, thinly sliced
¼ teaspoon chili flakes
2 scallions, thinly sliced, white and green parts separated
1½ tablespoons white miso paste
juice of ¼ lemon
ground black pepper, to taste
a pinch of sea salt flakes

1. Melt 1 tablespoon (½oz) butter in a large skillet over medium heat. Once melted, turn the heat up and sauté the mushrooms, seasoning them well with salt and pepper, for about 3–4 minutes until fully cooked. Transfer the mushrooms to a plate and set aside.

2. Bring a large pot of salted water to a boil and cook your tagliatelle until just before al dente (so about 3 minutes less than the package directions). Reserve about 1 cup (8fl oz) of the starchy pasta water.

3. While the pasta is cooking, make the sauce. Melt the remaining butter in the skillet over low heat, then fry the garlic, chili flakes and white parts of the scallions for 2–3 minutes until fragrant, and the scallions have softened.

4. In a bowl, combine the miso paste with ⅔ cup (5fl oz) of the starchy noodle water, whisking until you have a smooth paste. Add this to the pan and mix until combined. Then, using tongs, transfer the tagliatelle from the water straight into the pan. Give the noodles a really good toss until fully coated in the miso mixture, adding more noodle water as needed, until the noodles have absorbed the liquid and is fully cooked, and the sauce is glossy.

5. Once the sauce has thickened, take the pan off the heat and stir through the lemon juice, the green parts of the scallion and the cooked mushrooms, then serve with a good sprinkle of black pepper and a pinch of salt.

TIP

Use vegan butter to make this dish 100% vegan!

Asian-style "Spaghetti & Meatballs"

This is basically what you would get if stir-fried noodles and spaghetti and meatballs had a baby. Udon noodles are the perfect vessel, because they are quite sturdy and have a lovely chew to stand up to the Asian-inspired pork meatballs, flavored with Chinese five spice, garlic, and chili. And, rather than a standard tomato sauce, this is packed with all the aromatics (soy, sesame oil, rice wine vinegar) and marries everything together superbly. It's salty, slightly sweet, fragrant, and utterly delicious.

for the meatballs

4½ cups (17½oz) ground pork (I use lean, 5% fat pork but any should do)

5 scallions, finely sliced (use only the green parts reserving the white parts for the sauce), plus 1 extra to garnish

3 garlic cloves, finely chopped

1in piece of fresh ginger, grated

1½ teaspoons Chinese five spice

½ teaspoon fine sea salt

2 tablespoons light soy sauce

1 tablespoon dark soy sauce

1½ tablespoons sesame oil

1 tablespoon rice wine vinegar

½ teaspoon chili flakes

½ teaspoon ground white pepper

½ teaspoon ground black pepper

coconut or avocado oil, for frying

for the sauce

5 scallions, finely sliced (white parts only, see above)

6 garlic cloves, finely chopped

¼ teaspoon chili flakes (optional)

2 tablespoons tomato paste

4 tablespoons rice wine vinegar

2 tablespoons light soy sauce

1⅔ cups (14fl oz) chicken broth (use 1 stock cube)

2 tablespoons tomato ketchup

1 teaspoon maple syrup

6 teaspoons sesame oil

4 x 5½oz nests udon noodles (I use precooked, vacuum packed noodles)

1. Preheat the oven to 425°F/200°C fan/gas mark 7.

2. First make the meatballs. In a large bowl, combine all the ingredients and use your hands to mix everything together really well. When combined, take heaping teaspoons of the mixture and roll these into balls. You should end up with 16.

3. Heat 1 tablespoon oil in a large ovenproof skillet over medium heat and, once hot, flash-fry the meatballs for 1–2 minutes, just to get some color, then transfer the pan to the oven and bake for 10 minutes, until fully cooked and the juices run clear.

4. Now, for the sauce. Use a slotted spoon to remove the meatballs from the pan, and set these aside, leaving the juices in the pan. Place the pan back over low heat and add the whites of the scallions, along with the garlic and chili flakes, if using. Fry for 3–5 minutes, until the onions have softened, then add the tomato paste and fry this off for a few minutes until darkened.

5. Next, add the rice wine vinegar to the onion mixture to deglaze the pan, and give everything a good mix. Then, add the soy sauce, chicken broth, ketchup, maple syrup, and half the sesame oil. Mix well to combine, bring to a simmer, and then cook for a few minutes until the sauce has reduced slightly.

6. Submerge the noodles in the sauce and cook for about 2 minutes until separated. Then stir gently, and continue to cook over low heat until the noodles have soaked up most of the sauce, and they look glossy. Finally, add in the meatballs, toss well to combine and drizzle over the remaining sesame oil. Garnish with a finely sliced scallion and enjoy!

TIPS

If you are using dried or frozen udon noodles, simply cook these separately per package directions in salted water, drain, and then add them to the sauce in step 6.

There is not a binding agent in the meatballs, as I love to break them up into the noodles to eat them—however, if you want more sturdy meatballs, feel free to add an egg to the mixture.

Pasta, Rice, & Noodles

3

Comfort Food & Curries

Garbanzo Bean & Potato Curry

What I love about garbanzo bean curries is that many of them (like this one) are vegan, and you wouldn't even notice! I made this one in the tent during the *Great British Baking Show* final and it went down a storm! It's fragrant and slightly spicy but the key ingredient is, in fact, tomato ketchup, as it adds a sweetness and slight tanginess that balances everything out perfectly. The cilantro and red onion, which get stirred through right at the very end, also provide a lovely freshness and really add another dimension to the curry.

2 tablespoons coconut oil, for frying
10 large fresh curry leaves (or more if leaves are small)
1 teaspoon black mustard seeds
1 teaspoon cumin seeds
1 medium brown onion, finely diced
5 garlic cloves, finely chopped
1in piece of fresh ginger, grated
¼ teaspoon ground turmeric
1 tablespoon tomato paste
2 level tablespoons garam masala
2 x 14oz cans garbanzo beans, drained
2 medium white baking potatoes, peeled and diced (scant 1 cup diced)
1 teaspoon superfine sugar or 2 teaspoons jaggery
1 teaspoon fine sea salt
4 tablespoons tomato ketchup

to garnish

1 red onion finely diced
1 large bunch of fresh cilantro, finely diced (including stems)

1. Gently heat the oil in a large pan over low heat until melted, then fry the curry leaves, mustard seeds, and cumin seeds until fragrant, for about 2 minutes, making sure not to burn these as they will turn bitter. Add the onion with a pinch of salt and fry until browned. This does take about 30 minutes but is key to adding depth of flavor to the curry.

2. Add the garlic, ginger, turmeric, tomato paste, and garam masala, and fry until fragrant, for another 3–5 minutes.

3. Add the garbanzo beans and diced potato and mix these in the spices until well coated. Pour in 1⅔ cups (14fl oz) water and add the sugar, salt, and ketchup. Bring to a simmer, cover with a lid, and cook over low heat for 30–35 minutes until the potatoes are cooked through and the curry has thickened.

4. Remove the curry from the heat and stir through the diced red onion and chopped cilantro.

5. Serve with rice or chapatis and enjoy!

Soy & Herb Roast Chicken

I love roast chicken as much as the next person; however, it can often be bland and dry. In my opinion, everything comes down to the marinade, so here I'm sharing with you my favorite roast chicken recipe that is guaranteed to pack a flavor punch every time, as well as remaining incredibly juicy. It's herby, slightly sweet, aromatic, and with a lovely savory hit that comes from the soy sauce. And for any cilantro-haters out there, when it hits the oven, the flavor really mellows, and even my cilantro-hating sister loved it, so I hope this converts you! Also, something magical happens with this chicken—even though it is covered with parchment paper for the whole cooking process, the skin somehow browns perfectly and ends up crispy every time!

1 whole 4½lb chicken

for the marinade

5 garlic cloves
2 tablespoons light soy sauce
juice of ½ lime
1in piece of fresh ginger, grated
3 tablespoons olive oil
1 tablespoon honey
½ teaspoon ground black pepper
a good pinch of fine sea salt
1 large bunch of cilantro

1. Preheat the oven to 375°F/170°C fan/gas mark 5.

2. Place all the marinade ingredients in a food processor or blender and blitz to a smooth paste.

3. Using your hands, rub the marinade all over the chicken, inside and out, then either cover and place in the refrigerator to marinate for a few hours, or bake immediately.

4. When you are ready to roast, arrange the chicken in a large roasting pan or Dutch oven and cover with parchment paper, then secure with some string. Place in the oven and cook for 1 hour 40 minutes, until the skin is golden and the meat is cooked (a meat thermometer should read 180°F or, if you pierce the breast with a skewer, the juices should run clear and not be pink.

5. Remove the string and parchment paper, then turn the chicken upside down (resting on the breast) and let rest, covered, for 20 minutes, to allow the juices to run into the breast and keep it juicy. Then carve, and pour all those lovely juices all over the top.

6. I love serving this with some roast potatoes (try the Spicy Korean-inspired Smashed Potatoes on page 110) and veggies.

Char Siu Pulled Pork

Succulent, melt-in-the-mouth pulled pork goes well with just about everything, and this char siu marinade takes it to a whole new level. However, my big tip here is patience—it's a one-pot wonder—and you must sit back for a few hours as this slow-cooks away. The longer you leave it, the more tender your pork will be.

3¼lb boneless pork shoulder
3 medium brown onions, quartered
1 beef stock cube, dissolved in ½ cup (4fl oz) water (or ½ cup/4fl oz beef broth)

for the marinade

2 tablespoons honey
3 tablespoons plum sauce
8 tablespoons oyster sauce
3 tablespoons light soy sauce
1 tablespoon dark soy sauce
3 tablespoons ketchup
5 garlic cloves, finely chopped
1in piece of fresh ginger, grated
1½ teaspoons Chinese five spice
2 teaspoons sesame oil
¼ teaspoon ground black pepper
¼ teaspoon fine sea salt

1. In a large bowl, combine all the ingredients for the marinade and whisk well to combine.

2. Take the pork shoulder and, with a sharp knife, make some light slashes in the skin to help the marinade penetrate the meat. Using your hands, coat the meat in the marinade, covering every visible area of it.

3. At this point, you can cover the meat, refrigerate, and marinate for 2 hours (or up to 24 hours if you wish). However, you can also make this without marinating and it works perfectly!

4. Once ready to cook, transfer the pork and marinade to a large heavy pan. Arrange the pork skin-side up and tuck the onion slices underneath. This will add flavor but also prevent the pork from burning. Pour the beef broth over the top, then cover with a lid and place the pan over low heat. Let cook for 4 hours, stirring every hour and basting the pork in the liquid.

5. After 4 hours, use two forks to check if the meat can be easily pulled apart. If there is some resistance in the meat, put the lid back on and cook for another 30 minutes, until the meat can be shredded easily.

6. Once cooked, lift out the piece of pork and use two forks to shred the meat. Keep the pan with the juice over medium heat, simmering away, to reduce and concentrate. (If you wish, you can skim off the fat on the surface with a slotted spoon.)

7. Return the shredded meat to the pan and stir well to combine. Serve however you like (see Tips) and enjoy!

TIPS

You can have this with rice, in a wrap or bao buns, but my recommendation is to serve it in toasted brioche burger buns, with my Asian Slaw on page 84 and some wasabi mayo (simply mix 5 tablespoons mayo with 1 teaspoon wasabi and a squeeze of lime). It will be the best burger you have ever had!

This can also be cooked in a slow cooker.

Goan Egg Caldine Curry

This book would be incomplete without a few of my favorite Goan curries, and Egg Caldine is, hands down, one of the very best and also one of the simplest to make! The blend of aromatic spices with creamy coconut, sweet jaggery, and slightly tart tamarind captures the balanced flavor profile of traditional Goan cooking that I love so much. I vividly remember my mum making this when I was younger, and as soon as I could smell the coconut and cumin, I knew exactly what was bubbling away on the stove. And, for me, the best part was the okra (which I called lady fingers) that would soak up that lovely sauce and become soft and chewy.

5 extra-large eggs
4 garlic cloves, finely chopped
2 tablespoons (1oz) finely grated fresh ginger
2 teaspoons fine sea salt, plus a pinch
2 tablespoons coconut oil, for frying
2 medium onions, sliced
1 teaspoon ground turmeric
½ teaspoon ground cumin
¼ teaspoon ground black pepper
1 x 14oz can full-fat coconut milk
3 thin green chilis/Indian finger chilis sliced in half (double this if you like your curry spicy)
1 teaspoon jaggery (you can use coconut sugar or regular sugar if you don't have jaggery)
1 teaspoon tamarind concentrate
5¼oz frozen okra
white rice or chapatis, to serve

TIPS

You can also use fresh okra instead of frozen okra. However, this takes longer to cook, so I suggest frying the fresh okra in a separate pan until fully cooked and softened, and then add it to the curry with the eggs.

Swapping the eggs for tofu keeps this 100% vegan.

Learn more about tamarind concentrate in My Pantry Ingredients (page 10).

1. Place the eggs in a pan, cover with cold water and bring to a boil over medium heat. Cook for 10 minutes, then transfer to a bowl of ice-cold water and set aside while you make the curry.

2. Using a pestle and mortar, bash the garlic, ginger, and salt together to form a paste.

3. Heat the coconut oil in a large skillet over low–medium heat, then fry the onions with a pinch of salt until browned. Patience is a virtue here—this can take a while (up to 45 minutes), but it really is key to add flavor to your curry.

4. Add the turmeric, cumin, pepper, and ginger and garlic pastes, and fry this for another 5 minutes until fragrant.

5. Pour in the coconut milk and then add ¾ cup (7fl oz) water to the can and swirl it around, then pour this into the pan. Add the chilis, along with the jaggery or sugar, then turn up the heat and simmer for a couple of minutes to thicken slightly. Once thickened, add the tamarind paste and mix until dissolved.

6. Turn down the heat, add the frozen okra, cover with a lid and cook for 5 minutes.

7. Finally, remove the shells from the eggs, then slice them in half lengthwise. Place them in the curry, fully submerged. At this point, taste the curry and season to taste adding a little more salt, chili, tamarind, and sugar as needed. Serve with white rice or chapatis.

Lamb Shawarma Loaded Fries

Okay, brace yourselves for this one. The name of this dish alone gets my mouth watering. I love lamb shawarma—that spice mix is so warm and comforting, and so balanced that it marries perfectly with juicy lamb. Now, just imagine that spiced lamb, shredded apart and sprinkled over some French fries, and lathered in garlic sauce. Well, stop wasting time imagining when you can make it!

This definitely isn't the traditional method of cooking the lamb, as I've opted to slow roast the whole shoulder, which guarantees juicy lamb every time. Plus, it creates a great, show-stopping centrepiece if you're making this for guests. What makes this dish extra special is that it really gets the most out of the spice mix—it not only seasons the lamb but also the chunky fries, which means that every single element of this dish is bursting with flavor. Of course, if you're short on time, you can use a package or canned shawarma spice mix, but my method allows you to really bring out the flavors of the spices, by toasting the whole seeds before blitzing them down.

2½lb boneless lamb shoulder (you can also use a lamb leg too, see Tip on page 70)
1 vegetable stock cube
10 pickled chilis, to garnish

for the shawarma marinade*

5 cardamom pods
½ teaspoon kashmiri chili powder
¼ teaspoon ground nutmeg
1 teaspoon ground cinnamon
1 teaspoon paprika
1 teaspoon cumin seeds
2 teaspoons coriander seeds
1 teaspoon ground black pepper
5 whole cloves
1 teaspoon fine sea salt
1 teaspoon dried oregano
1 tablespoon garlic powder
3 garlic cloves
3 tablespoons olive oil

* If using a packaged schwarma spice mix, replace the first 9 ingredients with 5 tablespoons of spice mix.

Continued overleaf >>

1. First, make the shawarma marinade. In a large, dry skillet, add all the spices and toast over low heat for 5–7 minutes, until fragrant. Transfer these to a food processor or pestle and mortar, along with the salt, oregano, and garlic powder and grind to a fine powder.

2. Put 1½ tablespoons of this mixture in a bowl and set aside for seasoning the fries.

3. To the remaining spice mixture, add the garlic cloves and olive oil and blend to a paste. Rub this marinade all over the lamb until well coated, then place in a large, Dutch oven (with a lid) and set in the refrigerator to marinate for a minimum of 1 hour, or overnight.

4. When ready to cook, preheat the oven to 350°F/160°C fan/gas mark 4. Dissolve the stock cube in 2 cups (17fl oz) warm (not hot) water, then pour over the lamb. Cover tightly with the lid, then transfer to the oven for 3 hours, during which you should baste the meat in the cooking liquid about three times.

5. After this time, the meat should pull apart easily with two forks. If it still feels a bit tough, simply replace the lid, return to the oven and cook for another 30 minutes, then check again. When cooked to your liking, remove the lamb from the juices, and pull it into strips using two forks.

6. While the lamb is cooking, start preparing the fries. Heat the 7 tablespoons oil in a large roasting pan in the oven. While it is heating, place the fries in a large, heavy pan filled with cold, heavily salted water. Bring this to a boil, then cook over medium heat for 10–15 minutes, until the fries are partially cooked but still firm and not too soft around the edges. Drain.

Continued overleaf >>

for the fries

2¾lb white baking potatoes (5 large), sliced into chunky fries
7 tablespoons canola, avocado, or coconut oil
1 red bell pepper, thickly sliced
1 green bell pepper, thickly sliced
2 red onions, cut into large wedges
1 tablespoon olive oil
2 tablespoons malt vinegar

for the garlic sauce

⅔ cup (5¼oz) Greek yogurt
3 garlic cloves, grated
juice of ½ lemon
¼ teaspoon fine sea salt
10 mint leaves, finely chopped
pinch ground black pepper

for the pickled onions

1 red onion, finely sliced
juice of 1 lime

7. Place the drained fries back in the pan along with the peppers, onions, olive oil, vinegar, and 1 tablespoon of the reserved spice mix, and toss well to ensure everything is coated.

8. Carefully transfer the chip mixture to the hot, oiled roasting pan (ensuring they are not overlapping) and bake for 1 hour, rotating the pan and flipping the fries halfway through. Once the fries are cooked and golden around the edges, with a soft, fluffy interior, sprinkle over the remaining ½ tablespoon spice mix and give the fries a final toss.

9. Now make the garlic sauce. Put all the ingredients for the sauce in a small bowl and mix well to combine.

10. For extra zing and texture, make quick pickled onions. Simply add the lime juice to the red onion slices in a bowl and use your hands to scrunch them together, which will hasten the pickling process. Leave these to pickle for at least 30 minutes.

11. To assemble, spread the fries out on a large serving dish and sprinkle the pulled lamb over them. Drizzle the garlic sauce on top, sprinkle with pickled onions and pickled chilis, and then dig in.

TIPS

You can make a gravy with the leftover lamb juices: pour them into a pan, scrape off the fat and then cook down, stirring in 1 tablespoon of cornstarch.

If lamb shoulder is not available, a leg of lamb works perfectly too. Cook a 5lb leg for a total of 4½ hours, use scant 3 cups (24fl oz) water with 2 stock cubes, and double the amount of shawarma marinade.

"Even on their own, spices are punchy, bold, and individual. But, by combining multiple, you create an absolute flavor powerhouse, with a completely new flavor profile."

Lily Nana's Pickle Chicken Curry

For anyone who's followed my journey so far, this Goan curry may be familiar. It earned me the coveted "Hollywood Handshake" and Star Baker in the *Great British Baking Show* tent. So basically, this curry is a bit of magic.

It's called "pickle chicken" because of the high vinegar content. Vinegar is prominent in Goan cuisine (vindaloo is a well-known example)—and in this curry, the tanginess of the vinegar is offset with sweet flavors coming from the sweet potato and tomato ketchup, which may sound very unconventional but, trust me, it works. It would typically be made with coconut vinegar from the coconut palms in Goa, but I now make this with apple cider vinegar, which is readily available everywhere, and it works perfectly.

My late great grandmother, Lily Nana, used to make this curry in Bombay and she passed on the unwritten recipe to my late grandma, who passed it to my mom, who passed it to me. It's one that I've learned how to make by eye as a written recipe has never existed...until now! I really hope you enjoy a taste of Lily Nana's magic.

2 tablespoons extra virgin coconut oil, for frying

2 medium brown onions, finely sliced

1½ teaspoons ground coriander powder

5 teaspoons kashmiri chili powder

4 garlic cloves, grated/minced

8 skinless, boneless chicken thighs (1lb 5oz), diced

2 teaspoons fine sea salt

½ teaspoon ground black pepper

5 tablespoons tomato ketchup

6 tablespoons apple cider vinegar

2 small sweet potatoes, peeled and diced into small cubes

white rice, to serve

1. Heat the oil in a large pan over medium heat and fry the onions with a pinch of salt until browned. This can take 30–45 minutes, but patience is a virtue here.

2. Add the ground coriander, chili, and garlic, and fry until fragrant, for about 2 minutes. Add the chicken, season with salt and pepper and fry for about 5 minutes, until the chicken has browned.

3. Add the ketchup and apple cider vinegar and stir to ensure everything is well combined. Add the sweet potato and stir again. Cover with a lid and cook over low heat for 20 minutes, stirring now and again.

4. Remove the lid and cook down for another 5–10 minutes, until the curry has thickened, the chicken has cooked through and the potatoes are fully cooked and can be speared with a fork. Taste the curry and season to taste if needed. Serve with white rice.

TIP

You can swap the chicken for firm tofu to make this completely vegan.

Red Thai Chicken Pie

I love a good comforting pie—they are quintessentially British—but as I also love using fresh, vibrant flavors taken from international cuisines, out came this creation: my Red Thai Chicken Pie. Please don't be intimidated—there are lots of shortcuts in this recipe to make it as simple as possible. For example, some store-bought curry pastes are actually really good, so all we're going to do is spruce it up slightly with fresh lemongrass, fish sauce, and a hint of maple syrup to balance out the spiciness. We're also using ready-made puff pastry and, by layering in a little curry-flavored butter, you end up with an even flakier and more flavor-packed pastry, with minimal effort!

4 tablespoons coconut oil, for frying

1 large brown onion, thickly sliced into strips

1 leek, finely sliced

3 garlic cloves, finely chopped

6 scallions, cut horizontally into thirds

1in piece of fresh ginger, finely grated

8 skinless, boneless chicken thighs (1lb 5oz), cut into chunks

2 tablespoons good quality red Thai curry paste

2 tablespoons all-purpose flour

6oz baby corn, cut diagonally into thirds

3½oz sugar snap peas, cut diagonally into thirds

4 cups (9oz) chestnut or shiitake mushrooms, cut into quarters

1 x 14oz can full-fat coconut milk

2 tablespoons fish sauce

1 tablespoon maple syrup

1 stick lemongrass

a good pinch of fine sea salt and ground black pepper

for the puff pastry lid

1 heaping teaspoon Thai curry paste

4 tablespoons (2¼oz) unsalted butter, at room temperature

1 x 12oz ready-rolled puff pastry

1 egg (for egg wash)

2 tablespoons sesame seeds

1. Gently melt half the coconut oil in a large pan over low–medium heat, then fry the onion for a minute or two until softened. Add the leek and fry for another minute. Add the scallions, garlic, and ginger, and fry until soft, another 2 minutes. Transfer this mixture to a dish and set aside.

2. Add the remaining coconut oil to the pan and brown the chicken for about 5 minutes. Add the leek and onion mixture back in, along with the curry paste, stir to coat and fry for a couple of minutes until fragrant.

3. Sprinkle over the flour to coat everything and fry for 5 minutes. Add the vegetables, coconut milk (reserving the can), fish sauce, and maple syrup and mix to combine. Bash the lemongrass with a pestle to release its aromas, then add this to the pan and give everything a good stir. Season with salt and pepper.

4. Transfer the mixture into a 9½in-wide dish and let cool down to room temperature, then place in the refrigerator.

5. At this point, preheat the oven to 425°F/200°C fan/gas mark 7. Now prepare the puff pastry. In a bowl, mix 1 heaping teaspoon curry paste with the butter and beat until well combined. Roll out the puff pastry and spread this mix over one half of the pastry, then fold the dry side over the buttered side and roll this out to be slightly larger than the size of your Dutch oven.

6. Chill the pastry in the refrigerator for 10 minutes, to allow the butter layer to harden, then lay the pastry over the Dutch oven and fold any overhang inside the rim of the dish. 7. Beat the egg with any remaining coconut milk in the can and brush lightly over the pastry. Sprinkle over the sesame seeds and cut a small cross in the middle of the pastry, to allow some of the steam to escape.

8. Bake the pie in the oven for around 30 minutes, until the pastry has puffed up and is a golden brown color. Slice and serve. Just don't forget to remove the lemongrass after slicing.

"There is something so magical about combining two top-tier comfort foods. That's why a curry-filled pie is one of my all-time favorite things to make."

Salads & Veggies

Garlic Green Beans with Crispy Garbanzo Beans

I love green beans and I've always been fascinated by the way they are cooked at Thanksgiving—usually in a Dutch oven with some fried onions or shallots. So, here I've taken inspiration from my wonderful friends across the pond but added extra texture with crispy roasted garbanzo beans and nutty sesame seeds. Also, unlike the conventional Dutch oven, we're tossing the green beans in a wok to get some lovely char for even more flavor, which balances out perfectly against the maple and garlic.

for the crispy garbanzo beans

1 x 14oz can garbanzo beans
  (1¾ cup/8½oz drained)
2 tablespoons olive oil
2 teaspoons garlic powder
½ teaspoon paprika
½ teaspoon fine sea salt
½ teaspoon ground black pepper
3 tablespoons sesame seeds

for the green beans

2 tablespoons coconut oil, for frying
10½oz green beans, cut into thirds
1 red onion, thinly sliced
5 garlic cloves, thinly sliced
½ teaspoon chili flakes
½ teaspoon fine sea salt
¼ teaspoon ground black pepper
2 teaspoons sesame oil
3 teaspoons maple syrup
juice of ¼ lemon

1. Preheat the oven to 425°F/200°C fan/gas mark 7.

2. Drain the garbanzos and pat dry with paper towels, then tip into a large roasting pan and season with olive oil, garlic powder, paprika, salt, pepper, and sesame seeds. Use your hands to mix everything together, ensuring every garbanzo bean is coated in the spiced oil.

3. Place the pan in the oven and bake for 30 minutes, rotating the pan and tossing the garbanzos halfway through. Once baked, they should be golden and crisp.

4. Meanwhile, make the green beans. Melt the coconut oil in a wok over medium heat. Add the green beans and red onion and fry for 5 minutes, until the onion has softened. Add the garlic, chili flakes, salt, and pepper, and fry for another 10 minutes.

5. Drizzle over the sesame oil, maple syrup and lemon juice. Give everything one final toss to combine. Finally, mix in the crispy garbanzos and serve immediately.

TIP

If you are making this in advance, keep the roasted garbanzo beans in a separate, airtight container, and toss these through the green beans just before serving, so that they stay crunchy.

Charred Corn Salsa

I love a good zingy salsa and this one is a real taste of sunshine! The charred corn provides a lovely smoky sweetness, with caramelized notes that pair so well with the fresh lime. We've also got some creamy feta for that saltiness, pickled red onions for some tartness, jalapeños for a bit of heat and cilantro to add a freshness that really lifts the dish.

for the pickled onions

2 small red onions, finely diced
juice of 2 limes (juice separately)

1 tablespoon avocado or canola oil, for frying
3½ cups (1lb 5oz) drained canned corn (or 6 corn on the cob—see Tip)
½ teaspoon fine sea salt
20 canned red (or green) jalapeños, finely chopped
½ teaspoon smoked paprika
½ teaspoon regular paprika
7oz feta
a large bunch of cilantro, finely chopped (including stalks)

1. Place the diced onion in a small bowl and cover with the juice of 1 lime. Scrunch it together with your hands to help the onions pickle faster, then set aside.

2. Heat the oil in a cast-iron skillet over high heat. Once the oil is hot, add the corn with the salt and fry for 7–10 minutes until slightly charred, then remove from the heat and set aside.

3. Once the corn has cooled down, place it in a large bowl, along with the diced jalapeños, smoked paprika, and regular paprika, and mix well to combine.

4. Crumble the feta into the corn mixture and sprinkle over the chopped cilantro. Add in the pickled onions, including the pickling juices, and finally the juice of the remaining lime.

5. Give everything a really good toss to combine before eating. This is perfect as a side salad to serve alongside some grilled fish or chicken, or you can use it as a dip with some tortilla chips, or, you can toss through some cooked pasta and it makes a wonderful pasta salad!

TIPS

If using corn on the cob, brush the corn with oil and place these on a grill pan over medium-high heat for about 12 minutes, turning every couple of minutes, until charred and tender. Allow to cool a little, then use a sharp knife to slice off the corn kernels and proceed to make the rest of the salad from step 4, but remember to add in ½ teaspoon salt to the dressing.

Swap the feta for vegan cheese to make this 100% vegan.

Salads & Veggies

Asian Slaw with Peanut Dressing

In my opinion, coleslaw can be rather hit and miss. However, this one—which has no mayo!—is my favorite salad and I always make it for dinner parties because it has the perfect balance of flavors, is packed full of vibrant colors, and also happens to be vegan! The crunchy sugar snap peas and pickled pink radishes keep this salad fresh and light and the sweet, sharp, and salty flavors of the dressing bring it all to life.

9oz pink radishes, finely sliced on a mandoline

juice of 1¼ limes

¼ medium white cabbage (7½oz), finely sliced on a mandoline (about 2½ cups)

¼ medium red cabbage (7½oz), finely sliced on a mandoline (about 2½ cups)

4 small or 2 large carrots (6oz), cut into thin matchsticks

5¼oz sugar snap peas, finely sliced on a diagonal

5 scallions, thinly sliced into matchsticks

a bunch of cilantro, finely chopped

2 tablespoons toasted sesame seeds

for the dressing

juice of 1¼ limes

3 tablespoons sesame oil

2 tablespoons maple syrup

2 tablespoons crunchy peanut butter

2 tablespoons rice wine vinegar

1 teaspoon garlic powder

2 teaspoons light soy sauce

½ teaspoon ground black pepper

a pinch of fine sea salt

TIPS

If making this in advance, keep the dressing separate in the jar and pour over just before serving.

This is perfect on its own, or you can add in some form of protein like chicken or tofu, or even toss through some soba noodles. It also goes really well with my Char Siu Pulled Pork on page 64.

1. First, we're going to pickle the radishes. Place the radish slices in a small bowl and cover with lime juice, then set aside while you make the rest of the salad.

2. Place the white cabbage in a large bowl with the red cabbage. Add the carrots—they can be prepped using a julienne peeler, spiralizer, or sharp knife—and add to the bowl with the sugar snap peas, scallions, and cilantro. Use two large spoons to toss everything together until combined.

3. Now make the dressing. Place all the ingredients in a jar, secure the lid tightly and give it a really good shake. Pour the dressing all over the salad and give this a good mix. Add the radish, along with the pickling juices, and mix again well.

4. Place a dry skillet over low heat and toast the sesame seeds for about 5 minutes until nutty and fragrant.

5. Garnish the salad with the sesame seeds and a few cilantro leaves before serving.

Spiced Squash & Puy Lentil Salad

If you think that salads are one-dimensional, I guarantee that this one will change your mind. With sweet and spicy roasted red onions and squash, nutty Puy lentils, a creamy tahini dressing (which could be a dip in its own right), and a sprinkling of peppery arugula, it's a flavor and texture sensation. The hero spice is ras el hanout, which is a smoky and fragrant North African spice blend (see My Pantry Ingredients on page 10), but if you can't get your hands on it, you can use smoked paprika, which also works well.

for the roasted squash

1 small (1lb) butternut squash
2 red onions, sliced into wedges
3 teaspoons ras el hanout
2 teaspoons garlic powder
½ teaspoon chili flakes
½ teaspoon fine sea salt
½ teaspoon ground black pepper
3 tablespoons olive oil
1 tablespoon red wine vinegar
1 tablespoon maple syrup

for the lentils

1 x 8.8oz pouch (or 1½ cups) precooked
  Puy lentils
2 tablespoons olive oil, plus extra
  for drizzling
1 tablespoon maple syrup
a squeeze of lemon juice
1 teaspoon dried herbs (I like dried
  basil)
½ teaspoon garlic powder
fine sea salt and ground black pepper,
  to taste
1 x medium bag of arugula, to garnish

for the tahini dressing

3½ tablespoons tahini
juice of ½ lemon
1 tablespoon olive oil
scant 1 cup (7oz) Greek yogurt (or a
  dairy-free alternative)
1 teaspoon garlic powder
¼ teaspoon fine sea salt
¼ teaspoon ground black pepper

1. Preheat the oven to 400°F/180°C fan/gas mark 6.

2. First, prepare the butternut squash. With a sharp knife, top and tail it, slice it in half lengthwise and then scoop out the seeds and the stringy bits. Then cut each half into thick strips (which will look like half moons/semicircles). There's no need to peel the squash, as you can eat the skin!

3. Arrange the butternut squash and red onions on an roasting pan, then sprinkle over the ras el hanout, garlic powder, chili flakes, salt, pepper, olive oil, red wine vinegar and maple syrup. Use your hands to toss the vegetables in the flavorings until thoroughly coated.

4. Place the pan in the oven and roast for 30 minutes, rotating the pan halfway through and giving the vegetables a toss. Once cooked, the squash should be soft and pierce easily with a knife. Set aside to cool.

5. Place the puy lentils in a bowl. Add the olive oil, maple syrup, lemon juice, dried herbs, garlic powder, salt, and pepper, and give it a good stir to combine.

6. To make the tahini dressing, place all the ingredients in a bowl and whisk well to combine. Add 3 tablespoons of water and whisk again to loosen slightly.

7. To assemble, cover the bottom of a large, flat serving dish with arugula. Spoon the lentils into the center, then sprinkle the roasted squash and onions on top. Generously drizzle the tahini dressing all over and a little extra olive oil too, if you wish.

TIP

A dairy-free yogurt in the dressing makes this 100 percent vegan too!

Salads & Veggies

Five Spice Roasted Cauliflower

This d sh was first put together on a whim, when my mum called and asked me to make some veggies to go with a Chinese stir-fry for dinner. The only thing I had in the refrigerator was cauliflower and I'd never have thought that cauliflower would go with Chinese food. But then I thought, why don't I add some Chinese flavors to it? And the result was fantastic. My favorite way to cook cauliflower is to roast it, because it becomes so buttery and soft, and the leaves crisp up beautifully. With aromatic Chinese five spice, some soy sauce for rich, salty flavors, and a hint of sesame for nutty undertones, I really do believe that this will become your favorite side dish to go not just with Chinese dishes, but with almost any meal!

5 tablespoons olive oil

2 teaspoons light soy sauce

1 tablespoon rice wine vinegar

2 teaspoons Chinese five spice

1 teaspoon garlic powder

½ teaspoon fine sea salt

½ teaspoon ground black pepper

1 large cauliflower (including leaves), broken into small florets

1 tablespoon sesame oil

1 teaspoon toasted sesame seeds

1. Preheat the oven to 400°F/180°C fan/gas mark 6.

2. In a large baking pan, combine the olive oil, soy sauce, rice wine vinegar, Chinese five spice, garlic powder, salt and pepper and mix well to combine.

3. Add the cauliflower to the pan and use your hands to toss the florets and leaves in the marinade until well coated.

4. Place the pan in the oven and roast for 45 minutes, rotating the pan and tossing the cauliflower halfway through.

5. While the cauliflower is roasting, add 1 teaspoon sesame seeds to a dry skillet. Toast this on a low–medium heat for about 7 minutes until golden and nutty. Set aside.

6. Once roasted, the cauliflower should be soft enough to pierce easily with a sharp knife, and the leaves should be crisp and slightly charred.

7. Toss the cauliflower in the sesame oil and toasted sesame seeds before serving.

Grilled Peach, Goat Cheese, & Lentil Salad

I love a good sweet and salty combination and this salad really is the epitome of that. It is inspired by a salad I had in Paris years ago; I remember that the crunch of toasted hazelnuts, sharp goat cheese, and nutty lentils were such a fantastic combination. And here I'm adding a sweet dimension to the salad with grilled peaches and also some freshness coming from basil and dill. Grilling the peaches caramelizes the sugars and really concentrates the sweet flavors, and the slight char on the fruit adds a lovely smokiness too, which is perfectly balanced by the zingy lime in the dressing.

⅔ cup (5oz) green lentils, uncooked

1 vegetable stock cube

6½oz green beans, cut into thirds

¾ cup (3oz) skinless hazelnuts

8 large ripe but firm peaches, pitted and cut into 6 wedges

avocado or coconut oil, for brushing

4½oz firm goat cheese

a large handful (⅓ cup/¾oz) of fresh basil leaves

a large handful (¾oz) fresh dill

for the dressing

2½ tablespoons olive oil

juice of 1 lime

1 tablespoon rice wine vinegar

1 tablespoon honey

1 teaspoon garlic powder

½ teaspoon fine sea salt

½ teaspoon ground black pepper

TIPS

You can also save time by using 1⅔ cups (10oz) precooked green or Puy lentils.

Swap the goat cheese with vegan cheese, and swap the honey with agave syrup to make this vegan.

1. Place the lentils in a large pan with 2¾ cups (22fl oz) water. Bring to a boil, stir in the stock cube and cook for 15 minutes. Then, turn the heat down to a simmer, cover with a lid and cook for another 5 minutes. Turn off the heat and let stand in the steam for 5 minutes before removing the lid and fluffing up the lentils. Set aside to cool.

2. Place the green beans in a pan with about 2in of water, then cover with a lid and steam over low heat for 5 minutes (they should still retain some bite). Drain and set aside.

3. Now make the dressing. Place all the ingredients in a large bowl and whisk well to combine. Add the lentils and green beans directly into the dressing and toss well to coat.

4. Place the hazelnuts in a dry skillet over low heat and toast for about 10 minutes until golden and fragrant. Remove from the heat and bash lightly to break them up into smaller pieces (but not too fine).

5. Set a grill pan over high heat and brush with some oil. Place the peach wedges, cut-side down, on the pan and grill for 2–3 minutes on each side. Carefully remove the peaches from the grill—an offset rubber spatula works well to ensure that they don't stick to the pan.

6. Crumble the goat cheese into the salad, along with most of the hazelnuts and peaches, reserving a few for a garnish. Rip up the basil leaves, and chop up the dill, then add these to the salad (reserving a small handful) and mix again well to combine.

7. Serve the salad on a large, flat serving dish, and then sprinkle the remaining grilled peaches on top, along with an extra sprinkle of basil, dill, and hazelnuts.

Slow-roasted Harissa Carrots

I love carrots, but I really can't stand overcooked, soggy carrots. And when they're cooked without seasoning, they turn into a sweet mush—I find the whole concept so unsettling! So, I came up with this flavor-packed, sog-free recipe that my family now use all the time when we're doing a roast dinner. By roasting the carrots without parboiling them, they retain some crunch and the glaze really brings them to life. Spicy harissa, offset with the sweetness of honey and the sharpness of vinegar, gives these carrots the perfect flavor balance. You never have to eat bland and soggy carrots again!

6 medium carrots, cut diagonally into ovals, about ½in thick
2 tablespoons olive oil
2 tablespoons white wine vinegar
2 tablespoons harissa paste
1 teaspoon garlic powder
½ teaspoon fine sea salt
1½ tablespoons honey

1. Preheat the oven to 350°F/160°C fan/gas mark 4.

2. In a large baking pan, place the olive oil, white wine vinegar, harissa paste, garlic powder and salt and whisk well to combine.

3. Toss in the carrots and use your hands to ensure they are thoroughly coated in the flavorings.

4. Transfer the dish to the oven and bake for 1 hour 30 minutes until the carrots can be speared with a knife, rotating the pan and giving the carrots a mix halfway through.

5. Once baked, drizzle over the honey and toss once more before serving.

TIP

Swap the honey with agave syrup to make this vegan.

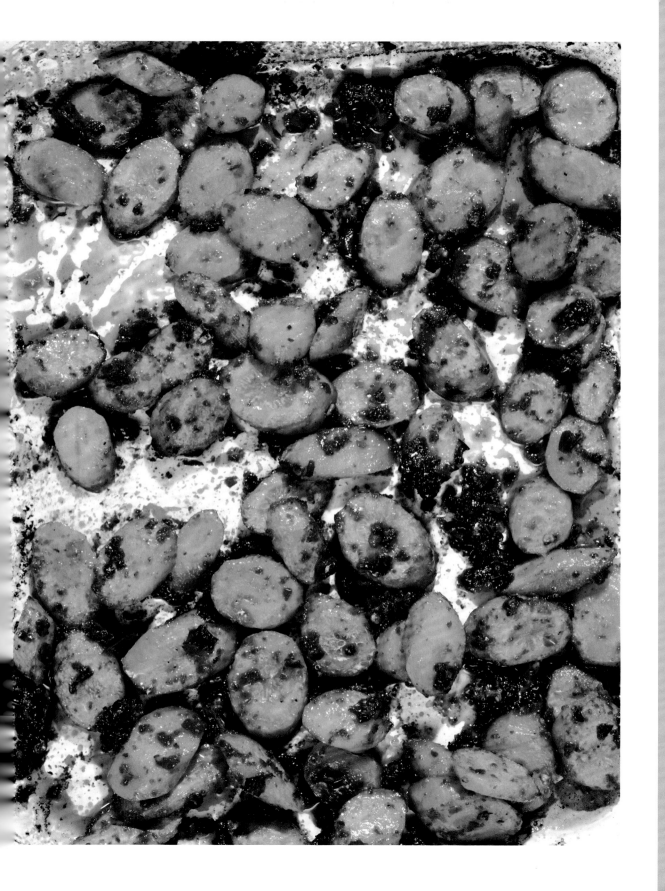

Small Plates & Dips

Salt & Pepper Halloumi Fries

Salt and pepper fries are one of my favorite Chinese takeaway dishes ever. The fries are tossed in a slightly spicy and peppery mixture, with Chinese five spice as the main seasoning, which lends a lovely, aromatic flavor. Here, I'm using halloumi instead of potato, coated in a seasoned cornstarch mixture to make them extra crispy on the outside, but lovely and soft inside. With a bit of maple syrup and soy for sweet and salty notes, paired with onions, garlic, and peppers for some freshness, this really is a taste sensation.

for the halloumi

8oz halloumi, cut into ¾in-thick fries
5 tablespoons melted coconut oil
2 tablespoons cornstarch
½ teaspoon Chinese five spice
2 teaspoons chili flakes
1 teaspoon garlic powder
¼ teaspoon ground ginger powder
½ teaspoon onion salt
½ teaspoon fine sea salt
½ teaspoon ground black pepper
¼ teaspoon ground white pepper

for the vegetables

4 tablespoons coconut oil
1 small brown onion, thinly sliced
1 scallion, finely sliced with the white and green parts separated
1 red bell pepper, sliced into thick strips
1 green bell pepper, sliced into thick strips
2 garlic cloves, finely chopped
1 teaspoon Chinese five spice
½ teaspoon ground black pepper
2 teaspoons light soy sauce
1 teaspoon maple syrup
juice of ½ lime

TIPS

The squeeze of lime at the end cuts through the richness perfectly, so make sure not to miss this out!

To make this vegan, swap halloumi for firm tofu.

1. Place the halloumi in a bowl, drizzle with 2 tablespoons melted coconut oil and toss to coat.

2. In a separate bowl, mix the cornstarch with all the spices and seasonings, then toss the halloumi in the mixture until completely coated.

3. Place 3 tablespoons of coconut oil in a large skillet over medium-high heat. Once the oil is hot, take each stick of halloumi and shake off any excess cornstarch, then carefully place in the hot oil and fry for 2–3 minutes on each side until crispy and golden. Transfer to a plate lined with paper towels and set aside.

4. Now cook the vegetables. Add a little more oil if needed, then add the onion, white parts of the scallion, the peppers, and the garlic. Toss in the oil and fry for about 30 seconds to 1 minute.

5. Add the five spice, pepper, soy sauce, and maple syrup, stir to combine, and fry for another 30 seconds. Then add back in the halloumi fries and toss to coat in the spices and mix with the vegetables.

6. Take the pan off the heat and stir through the lime juice and the green parts of the scallions. Serve warm and enjoy!

Korean-inspired Garlic Bread

This is not your average garlic bread. Gochujang really makes this sing, providing a bit of spice, but also a deep, peppery flavor. And for those who don't like a lot of spice, don't worry—the cream cheese softens the impact to create something that is very balanced. This is perfect as a starter, or you could top it with some salad and a bit of thinly sliced ham to create a delicious lunch.

1 large baguette
⅔ cup (2½oz) grated mozzarella
2 scallions, finely chopped,
   to garnish
1 tablespoon sesame seeds,
   to garnish

for the gochujang sauce
1 tablespoon gochujang
½ tablespoon honey
2 tablespoons rice wine vinegar

for the garlic butter
6 garlic cloves, finely chopped
1 stick (½ cup/4oz) unsalted butter,
   at room temperature
6 tablespoons (3oz) cream cheese
1 tablespoon gochujang
¼ teaspoon chili flakes
¼ teaspoon fine sea salt

1. Preheat the oven to 400°F/180°C fan/gas mark 6.

2. First make the gochujang sauce. Combine the ingredients in a small bowl and mix well to combine, then set aside.

3. To make the garlic butter, place all the ingredients in a bowl and mix until well combined.

4. Cut the baguette lengthwise down the middle so that you have long halves of bread (like an open sandwich). Divide the spiced butter mixture into two equal parts and spread evenly over each slice of bread. Arrange the bread on a large baking sheet, then place in the oven and bake for 10 minutes.

5. Remove from the oven and sprinkle the mozzarella over each slice, then return to the oven for another 10 minutes. Finally, switch the oven to the broil setting and broil under a high heat for 1 minute, watching the bread carefully, until the cheese is slightly golden.

6. Once baked, carefully remove the garlic bread, garnish with scallions and sesame seeds and cut into thin slices. Finally, drizzle with the gochujang sauce and enjoy warm.

"I vividly remember trying gochujang for the first time in South Korea, and being blown away by its complex flavor. When I got back to London I went straight to the supermarket to hunt it down."

Cheesy Olive Spiced Scones

These really are sublime. The warming ras el hanout spices (learn more in My Pantry Ingredients on page 10) offset the layers and layers of cheese and, with salty olive nuggets and a crunch of sesame on top, they're a cut above your regular scone. To pack in that cheesiness and retain the flakiness of the scone, we will be following a really simple laminating process—which is just folding the dough over twice, to create layers.

1 cup (4¼oz) grated cheddar
¼ cup (¾oz) grated Parmesan
1⅔ cups (7oz) all-purpose flour
2½ teaspoons baking powder
2½ teaspoons ras el hanout
1 teaspoon za'atar
½ teaspoon chili flakes
¾ teaspoon fine sea salt
scant ½ cup (3½oz) very cold (frozen if possible) unsalted butter, cut into cubes
scant ½ cup (1½oz) pitted black olives, diced
½ cup (4oz) buttermilk, cold
1 egg, beaten
4 tablespoons sesame seeds

TIPS

Freeze your flour if you can, and I recommend cutting your butter into cubes and freezing it before you start. If your butter is warm, you simply will not get flakiness in your scones, or a good rise. Essentially, you want to treat this like pastry—don't overwork it. If, at any point, you feel as though your dough is becoming warm and soft, simply place it in the refrigerator or freezer to cool down.

You can substitute the buttermilk with ½ cup (4fl oz) whole milk mixed with 1 teaspoon vinegar or lemon juice. If you are doing this, mix the milk and vinegar about 5 minutes before you need to use it and leave it in the refrigerator—it must be cold.

1. In a large bowl, mix the grated cheeses together, then set aside.

2. In another large bowl or stand mixer bowl place the flour, baking powder, ras el hanout, za'atar, chili flakes and salt and add in half the cheese mixture. Mix well to combine.

3. Add the cold butter cubes to the dry mixture, and use your fingertips to rub the butter into the flour—it should resemble slightly chunky bread crumbs. Add the black olives and mix to combine.

4. Next, slowly pour in the buttermilk, using a butter knife to stir this together (or a paddle attachment of a stand mixer). Mix until the ingredients just come together to form a shaggy dough. Tip onto a clean, floured counter and carefully push the dough together, without overworking it too much, until it forms a cohesive dough.

5. Using a floured rolling pin, roll out the dough into a rough rectangle, about 10in long and 4½in wide. Sprinkle over half the remaining cheese mixture and lightly press this into the dough. Now we want to create layers by folding over the dough. Pick up a short end and fold two-thirds over, then fold the remaining third back over the first fold, you should now have three layers. Turn the pastry 90 degrees, then roll out again. Sprinkle over the remaining cheese and repeat the folds as before. Finally, roll the dough out into a rectangle again and pat down to a thickness of 1–1¼in. You may need to chill your dough if it is becoming warm.

6. Use a sharp knife to cut the dough into 8 equal squares, then evenly space the scones on a lined baking sheet and either freeze them for 15 minutes or refrigerate for 45 minutes, for the butter to harden completely. While your dough is chilling, preheat the oven to 200°C fan/425°F/gas mark 7.

7. Once ready to bake, brush the tops lightly with beaten egg and generously sprinkle with sesame seeds.

8. Bake for 15 minutes (watching the color to make sure they do not brown too much), then rotate the pan, turn the oven down to 375°F/170°C fan/gas mark 5 and continue baking for another 10–12 minutes until the scones are perfectly golden, and achieve a good rise. I think these are best served warm, but they're perfect picnic food too!

Hoisin Duck "Sausage" Rolls

I feel I had a lightbulb moment when this idea came into my head. Duck pancakes are one of my favorite starters when I eat out. I just love the fact that, in a couple of bites, your mouth is filled with so many different flavor and texture sensations, each one packing a punch. So, I thought, why not turn this into a sausage roll—you add extra texture with the crispy puff pastry and lose the hassle of having to assemble the pancake. I should caveat that the name is slightly misleading as there's no actual sausage meat in this recipe; just duck and some pancetta! I really wanted the duck's flavor to shine and I hope you'll find that it works perfectly.

2 duck legs (16oz)
4 scallions, finely sliced
½ cup (3½oz) diced pancetta
13oz ready-rolled puff pastry
1 egg, beaten
black sesame seeds, to garnish

for the marinade

4 garlic cloves, grated
1in piece of fresh ginger, grated
2 teaspoons Chinese five spice
½ teaspoon chili flakes
2 teaspoons light soy sauce
2 teaspoons rice wine vinegar
½ teaspoon ground black pepper
¼ teaspoon fine sea salt
1 teaspoon olive oil

for the hoisin sauce

1 tablespoon dark soy sauce
2 tablespoons light soy sauce
2 tablespoons plum sauce
2 teaspoons rice wine vinegar
2 teaspoons sesame oil
2 tablespoons smooth peanut butter
1 tablespoon dark brown sugar
1 teaspoon garlic powder
½ teaspoon chili flakes
a pinch ground black pepper

TIP

Store any leftover hoisin sauce in an airtight jar and refrigerate for up to 3 weeks. If you're short on time, you can buy ready-made hoisin sauce.

1. Preheat the oven to 375°F/170°C fan/gas mark 5, if not marinating, otherwise preheat 10 minutes before cooking.

2. First make the marinade. Place all the ingredients in a bowl and mix well to combine.

3. Using a sharp knife, carefully score the duck skin in diagonal lines, then rub the marinade all over the duck, making sure to rub it inside the scored lines. You can then either leave the duck to marinate for a few hours or place it on a roasting pan immediately and cook it for 45 minutes.

4. Once cooked remove the duck from the oven and turn up the oven temperature to 425°F/200°C fan/gas mark 7.

5. Remove the duck from the bone, and two forks to shred the duck meat, fat, and skin into fine pieces. If the meat is still pink, don't worry as this will be going back in the oven. Once shredded, add the duck to a food processor along with the scallions and pancetta and pulse until almost smooth, similar to the consistency of sausage meat.

6. Next, make the hoisin sauce. Combine all the ingredients in a bowl and mix well. Spoon 4 tablespoons of the sauce into the shredded duck mixture and mix to combine.

7. Next, assemble your rolls. Ensure the duck is cool to the touch before assembling the pastry (it should be by now). Cut your sheet of puff pastry into four long strips crosswise (approximately 10 x 3½in) and spread ½ tablespoon of hoisin sauce over each piece. Divide the duck mixture into four and distribute it down the middle of each strip. Now fold over each pastry strip lengthwise, to enclose the meat and, using a fork, press down to seal tightly and create a pattern down each side. Cut each log into 8 pieces, 1½in long.

8. Brush beaten egg over each roll and sprinkle with a few sesame seeds. Arrange them on a lined baking sheet and, if your kitchen is warm and your pastry is getting warm and soft, place it in the freezer for about 10 minutes to firm up—this will help the pastry rise when you bake the rolls.

9. Bake in the oven for 20–25 minutes until the pastry has puffed up and is golden brown.

Roasted Grape, Honey, & Feta Crostini

This creation is heavily inspired by one of my favorite signature bakes in the *Great British Baking Show* tent. I had made a focaccia during Bread Week, with roasted grapes, sharp, salty feta, crunchy walnuts and fresh fennel. It went down a treat, and so I've transferred all of the same flavors and textures into crispy crostini—little bites of sweet and salty deliciousness.

I love the addition of fresh fennel, and I think it provides some lightness to cut through the rich cheese and roasted grapes. However, if you can't get your hands on any, you can leave it out, or add some fresh dill (which comes from the same family).

for the infused oil

3½ tablespoons (2fl oz) olive oil
2 garlic cloves, grated
½ tablespoon dried thyme

for the crostini

8½oz black seedless grapes (about 24 grapes)
7oz feta
10 walnuts, skin on
1 small baguette
1½ tablespoons runny honey
¼ fresh fennel bulb, thinly sliced (optional)
a bunch of fresh thyme
a pinch of fine sea salt and ground black pepper

1. Preheat the oven to 400°F/180°C fan/gas mark 6.

2. First make the infused oil. Place the olive oil in a small pan with the garlic and thyme and heat very gently over low heat for about 10 minutes, until the oil is sizzling and fragrant. Turn off the heat and set aside.

3. Arrange the grapes in a roasting pan and spoon 3 teaspoons of the infused oil over the top. Toss the grapes until they are coated, then place in the oven and roast for 20 minutes, until they are sizzling and the skins have shriveled slightly. Allow to cool, then slice each grape in half lengthwise.

4. Place the feta in a food processor with a splash of feta water (or a splash of milk if your feta does not have water), a good pinch of pepper and a tiny pinch of salt and blend until completely smooth.

5. Place the walnuts in a dry skillet over medium heat and toast for around 7 minutes until slightly browned and fragrant. Allow to cool slightly, then break into small pieces and set aside.

6. Slice the baguette diagonally into thin crostini slices (about ½in thick) and drizzle a teaspoon of the infused oil over each slice. Place these in a baking pan and toast in the oven for 7–10 minutes until crispy and golden, or alternatively cook on a grill pan over high heat for 4 minutes, flipping halfway through.

7. To assemble, spread 1 heaping teaspoon of whipped feta over each crostini and drizzle with honey. Top with about 4 grape halves and a sprinkle of fennel, crushed walnuts and fresh thyme leaves, and serve immediately.

TIP

To make this vegan, swap the feta for vegan cream cheese, and swap the honey for agave.

Dhokla-inspired Cornbread Muffins

Dhokla is a slightly sweet and savory snack from India that is almost like a light, steamed sponge cake, flavored with the most beautiful aromatic tempered spices. Now, while dhokla is usually made with garbanzo beans, it has always reminded me of cornbread, as both are soft, bouncy, slightly sweet and with a beautiful, vivid yellow color. So, I've decided to spice up the cornbread muffins we know and love to create a deliciously spiced snack, with flavors reminiscent of dhokla that is incredibly moreish. This is less sweet than your standard cornbread, because I find that the spices really sing when paired with more savory notes.

6 tablespoons coconut oil

1 teaspoon black mustard seeds

½ teaspoon cumin seeds

20 curry leaves

2 thin green chilis/Indian finger chilis, finely diced

1in piece of fresh ginger, grated

generous ½ cup (4½fl oz) whole milk, room temperature

1 teaspoon lemon juice

¾ cup (3oz) self-rising flour

1½ teaspoons baking powder

scant ½ cup (1¾oz) yellow fine or medium cornmeal

3 tablespoons (1½oz) granulated sugar

1 teaspoon fine sea salt

¼ teaspoon ground turmeric

¼ teaspoon chili powder

1 extra-large egg

1. Preheat the oven to 400°F/180°C fan/gas mark 6 and line a muffin pan with 6 muffin cases.

2. First, temper the spices. Melt the coconut oil in a pan over low heat. Add the mustard seeds, cumin seeds, curry leaves, chilies, and ginger, and cook for about 3 minutes until fragrant. Turn off the heat and stir for another 2 minutes.

3. Carefully transfer 6 curry leaves to a plate lined with paper towels and let crisp up (for the garnish). Pour the warm oil and spices into a medium bowl and set aside to cool down.

4. Pour the milk into a pitcher, stir through the lemon juice, then set aside to curdle slightly.

5. Place the flour, baking powder, cornmeal, sugar, salt, turmeric, and chili powder in a large bowl and whisk until combined.

6. Add the milk mixture to the cooled spiced oil and whisk in the egg.

7. Slowly pour the wet mixture into the dry mixture, whisking slowly until no lumps remain. Fill the muffin cases with the batter and bake in the oven for 18–20 minutes, until springy and a skewer comes out clean.

8. Garnish the muffins with the crispy curry leaves and enjoy with some butter, if you wish.

TIP

The key here is to temper the spices in coconut oil over low heat, to really bring out their flavors. Keep the heat low or the spices will burn and turn bitter.

Spicy Korean-inspired Smashed Potatoes

If you've never had smashed potatoes before, you're in for a treat. By smashing them halfway through roasting, you create a larger surface area, with little gnarly bits of potato that crisp up and provide such an incredible, crunchy texture. But these aren't just any smashed potatoes. They are Korean-inspired; coated in a spicy, slightly sweet and sticky gochujang glaze and sprinkled with chopped scallions for freshness, which takes them to the next level.

for the roast potatoes

6 tablespoons coconut or avocado oil
2¼lb baby potatoes
3 tablespoons olive oil
2 tablespoons rice wine vinegar
2 teaspoons garlic powder
1 teaspoon fine sea salt, plus extra
    for boiling
½ teaspoon ground black pepper

for the gochujang glaze

2 tablespoons gochujang
1 tablespoon honey
1½ teaspoons sesame oil
½ teaspoon garlic powder
pinch of fine sea salt and ground
    black pepper

to garnish

1½ tablespoons sesame seeds
2 scallions, finely diced
½ teaspoon chili flakes

1. Preheat the oven to 400°F/180°C fan/gas mark 6.

2. Heat the coconut or avocado oil in a large roasting pan in the oven.

3. Place the baby potatoes in a large pot of heavily salted water and bring to a boil. Once boiling, cook for 15 minutes, until they can be pierced with a sharp knife but still retain their shape. Drain.

4. Place the potatoes back in the pot along with the olive oil, rice wine vinegar, garlic powder, salt, and pepper. Cover with a lid and give the pan a good shake to toss the potatoes in the seasoning.

5. Remove the pan with the hot oil from the oven, then carefully add the potatoes to the pan and turn to coat in the hot oil. Roast for 15 minutes.

6. While the potatoes are roasting, make the glaze. Place all the ingredients for the glaze in a small bowl and mix to combine.

7. After 15 minutes, take out the potatoes, pour over the gochujang glaze and mix well until all the potatoes are coated. Then, either use a potato masher or the bottom of a jar (something heavy) to squash the potatoes and flatten them out on the pan.

8. Sprinkle over the sesame seeds and return the pan to the oven for another 15 minutes, then use a spatula to carefully flip them over, before baking for a final 10 minutes.

9. Garnish with the scallions and chili flakes.

TIP

Swap honey for agave to make this vegan.

Honey & Chipotle-baked Camembert with Homemade Croutons

I make this almost every time my friends come over because you just can't go wrong with melted, bubbling cheese. You can jazz up Camembert with so many different flavors but this one is my favorite: chipotle paste and honey, providing spicy and sweet notes that balance out the strong cheese perfectly. Paired with some quick and easy croutons (using up any leftover bread you have in the refrigerator), you have the ideal contrast of gooey and crunchy textures.

for the croutons

5 tablespoons olive oil
1 teaspoon garlic powder
1 teaspoon dried oregano
1 teaspoon paprika
½ teaspoon fine sea salt
½ teaspoon cayenne pepper
5 slices of white bread, cut into small triangles

for the camembert

1 x 9oz camembert in a wooden tray
1 tablespoon olive oil
2 garlic cloves, thinly sliced
1 tablespoon chipotle paste (add ½ tbsp extra if you like it spicy!)
2 tablespoons honey, plus extra for drizzling
a small handful of chives, finely chopped, for sprinkling

1. Preheat the oven to 375°F/170°C fan/gas mark 5.

2. In a large roasting pan, place the olive oil, garlic powder, oregano, and paprika, along with the salt and cayenne pepper and mix well to combine. Toss the bread triangles in the oil until well coated on both sides.

3. Place the pan in the oven for 15 minutes and cook, rotating halfway through, until the croutons are golden and crisp.

4. Meanwhile, prepare the camembert. Remove all the plastic packaging and place the cheese in the wooden container it comes in (most col). Using a sharp knife, crosshatch the surface of the camembert, taking care not to cut down to the bottom.

5. In a small bowl mix together the oil and sliced garlic, then take the garlic and wedge the slices into the cross-hatched slits until fully submerged. Mix together the chipotle paste and honey in the same bowl, then pour over the top of the camembert.

6. Place the cheese in a roasting pan and bake in the oven for 20 minutes, until the cheese has melted completely inside.

7. Remove from the oven, drizzle with a little extra honey and sprinkle over the chives. Mop up the camembert with the crispy croutons and enjoy!

SERVES 4–6 | PREP: 15 MINS | COOK: 45 MINS | VG/VeS |

Beet Tartare & Whipped Goat Cheese Dip

I love how sharp, creamy goat cheese pairs so well with sweet flavors, like figs, caramelized onions and, in this case, beets. I also discovered recently that, if you blitz soft goat cheese (which is a slightly milder version) in a food processor, it turns into a smooth, luscious spread, and so I created this stunning dip. The beet and honey are earthy and sweet, the lemon, dill, and balsamic vinegar add a fresh acidity and the toasted hazelnuts bring a beautiful buttery crunch. This dip is full of vibrant colors so will really get everyone's attention at the dinner table.

1 large (6oz) beet
5 garlic cloves, unpeeled
2 tablespoons olive oil
½ teaspoon thyme
¼ teaspoon fine sea salt
¼ teaspoon ground black pepper
⅓ cup (1¾oz) hazelnuts
crackers or crusty bread, to serve

for the goat cheese dip

5¼oz soft goat cheese
juice of ½ lemon
a pinch of ground black pepper
a pinch of fine sea salt

for the dressing

1 teaspoon olive oil
1 teaspoon balsamic vinegar
1 tablespoon honey, plus extra to serve
1 teaspoon garlic powder
a pinch of fine sea salt and ground black pepper
zest of 1 lemon
a handful of chopped dill fronds

TIPS

You can also use precooked beet to save some time. See notes in the recipe.

To make this vegan, swap goats cheese for vegan cream cheese, and honey for agave.

1. Preheat the oven to 400°F/180°C fan/gas mark 6.

2. Place the uncooked beet and garlic cloves on a piece of aluminum foil, drizzle with olive oil, and sprinkle over the thyme, salt, and pepper. Wrap up the beet and garlic tightly in the foil, place in a small ovenproof dish, then roast in the oven for 45 minutes, until the beet can be pierced easily with a knife. (If using precooked beet, then just proceed to roast the garlic.)

3. Place the hazelnuts in a roasting pan and toast in the oven for 10 minutes until golden. Allow to cool slightly before roughly chopping into small chunks.

4. To make the whipped goat cheese dip, place all the goat cheese, lemon juice, salt, and pepper in a small food processor. Peel the roasted garlic cloves and add these to the mix, then blitz to a smooth paste. Set aside.

5. Now, make the beet tartare. Place the olive oil, balsamic vinegar, honey, garlic powder, salt, and pepper in a bowl and whisk well to combine. Unwrap the roasted beet, peel off the skin, and then finely dice into very small cubes. Add these to the bowl along with the hazelnuts, lemon zest and dill (reserving a little of all three to garnish) and mix well to coat in the dressing.

6. Transfer the whipped goat cheese onto a plate and spread out with the back of a spoon. Add the beet tartare in a tall pile in the center and, finally, garnish with the reserved lemon zest, dill, and hazelnuts. Drizzle with a squeeze of honey and serve with crackers or crusty bread.

Edamame Hummus

My favorite bean, hands down, is the humble edamame. I guess it's because I love pan-Asian cuisine so much, where they feature everywhere, and they have a lovely nuttiness and slight sweetness that make them so moreish. So, I present to you, my edamame hummus, with an added crispy edamame topping that provides that bit of crunch and texture to contrast with the smooth hummus, as well as bursts of flavor.

for the crispy roasted edamame topping

⅓ cup (1¾oz) fresh or frozen edamame beans, out of their pods (if frozen, see Tip to prepare)
2 tablespoons olive oil
1 teaspoon garlic powder
¼ teaspoon chili flakes
¼ teaspoon fine sea salt
a pinch of ground black pepper
2 teaspoons white sesame seeds
2 sheets of crispy seaweed, finely chopped

for the hummus

¾ cup (3½oz) fresh or frozen edamame beans, out of their pods (if frozen, see Tip to prepare)
1 tablespoon olive oil
1 tablespoon sesame oil, plus extra to garnish
1 teaspoon fish sauce
juice of 1 lime
1 garlic clove
1 tablespoon tahini
¼ teaspoon fine sea salt
a pinch of ground black pepper

TIPS

If using frozen edamame beans, place them in a pan with ¼ cup (2fl oz) water over low heat. Cover with a lid and steam for 10 minutes, until cooked.

Swap the fish sauce for light soy sauce to make this vegan.

1. Preheat the oven to 375°F/170°C fan/gas mark 5.

2. First make the crispy roasted edamame topping. Place the ⅓ cup (1¾oz) edamame beans on a roasting pan with the olive oil, garlic powder, chili flakes, salt, pepper, and sesame seeds and use your hands to toss the beans in the marinade until well coated. Place the pan in the oven and roast for 20 minutes until crispy and golden, stirring the beans halfway through.

3. Once roasted, sprinkle with the crispy seaweed and toss together, then set aside while you make the hummus.

4. To make the hummus, place all the hummus ingredients in a blender along with ¼ cup (2fl oz) water and blitz until smooth.

5. To serve, transfer the hummus to a plate and spread out with the back of a spoon. Top with the crispy edamame topping and a drizzle of sesame oil and enjoy with crackers, bread, or flatbread.

1 Charred Scallion & Miso Pesto
2 Cheesy Baked Crab & Corn Dip
3 Beet Tartare & Whipped Goat
  Cheese Dip
4 Pea, Mint & Feta Dip
5 Edamame Hummus

4

5

Cheesy Baked Crab & Corn Dip

I love crab and corn soup—and it's just as – if not more – delicious turned into a cheesy dip. Please try and get your hands on fresh crabmeat (my local supermarket stocks this in the chilled section in tubs)—it includes the brown meat, which is as flavorful as a stock cube. I love to enjoy this dip with shrimp crackers but tortilla chips or crusty bread work so well too. Make this for your next dinner party and I assure you, everyone will go mad for it (in a good way)!

2 x large cans corn (3½ cups/20oz drained)

1 cup (7oz) cream cheese, softened

¼ cup (2fl oz) sour cream

¼ cup (2¼oz) mayonnaise

2 tablespoons fish sauce

1 tablespoon light soy sauce

1 teaspoon olive oil, for frying

5 large scallions, thinly sliced (white and green parts separated)

2 garlic cloves, finely chopped

1 teaspoon chili flakes

scant 1 cup (7oz) fresh crabmeat (including brown meat)

⅓ cup (1½oz) grated cheddar

⅔ cup (1¾oz) finely grated Parmesan

1 cup (3½oz) grated mozzarella

fine sea salt and ground black pepper

1. Preheat the oven to 400°F/180°C fan/gas mark 6.

2. Place half the corn in a food processor, along with the cream cheese, sour cream, mayonnaise, fish sauce, and soy sauce. Blitz until smooth and transfer to a bowl.

3. Heat the olive oil in a 10in ovenproof pan over low heat. Once warm, add the white scallion parts with the garlic and chili flakes and fry for 2–3 minutes until fragrant. Remove from the heat, and add to the blitzed corn mixture.

4. To this mixture, add in the remaining corn along with the crabmeat, cheddar, Parmesan, half the mozzarella and the green parts of the scallions. Season well with salt and pepper and mix thoroughly to combine.

5. Transfer the mixture back to the pan and flatten out with the back of a rubber spatula. Top with the remaining mozzarella, then place in the oven and bake for 20 minutes, until the cheese has melted and the mixture is bubbling.

6. Serve warm with shrimp crackers, tortilla chips or crusty bread.

TIP

If you have any leftover dip, this makes a delicious pasta sauce! Simply put the pan back on the stove until the dip is warm, and then add cooked pasta directly to the pan, with some pasta water to loosen it slightly and stir until combined.

Pea, Mint, & Feta Dip

I didn't know that one dip could have so many different flavor sensations... until now. This dip is salty, fresh, and tangy, thanks to the feta, mint, and lemon, which complement the sweet green peas. And for extra texture, we will be leaving half of the peas chunky for some bite. It's perfect to slather on your toast or to dunk your tortilla chips in. And the best part is that it all comes together in 10 minutes! Wins all round in my book.

¾ cup (3½oz) frozen peas
2 garlic cloves, lightly smashed
a large handful of mint leaves
   (about 50), plus extra to garnish
juice of ½ lemon
3½oz feta, plus extra for garnish
½ teaspoon ground black pepper
a pinch of fine sea salt
extra virgin olive oil, for garnish

1. Place the peas in a pan with 2 tablespoons water over a low heat. Cover with a lid and steam for 5 minutes until soft and plump.

2. Transfer half the peas to a food processor along with the rest of the ingredients and blitz until smooth.

3. Add in the remaining peas and pulse lightly—we want to leave these slightly chunky for texture.

4. Spoon the dip into a small bowl and garnish with fresh mint, a drizzle of olive oil and some more crumbled feta, if you like. Serve with tortilla chips and crudités, or spread over toast.

Charred Scallion & Miso Pesto

This is not a conventional pesto. Although, the word pesto simply means "to pound or to crush," which is the traditional way that pesto used to be prepared, with a pestle and mortar. Here, charred scallions provide an earthy and slightly bitter flavor, with fragrant cilantro, nutty toasted sesame seeds and sesame oil, miso paste for that umami undertone we know and love, and honey for some mellow sweetness. I love to stir this pesto through some pasta, garnished with crispy chili oil, or drizzle it over a steak, salmon, or grilled vegetables. Your options are endless.

5 scallions, trimmed
2 tablespoons olive oil
3 tablespoons sesame seeds
a large bunch of cilantro
2 garlic cloves, finely chopped
juice of 1 lime
2 teaspoons white miso
1 tablespoon sesame oil
a pinch of ground black pepper
3 teaspoons honey or agave (VeS)

1. Place a large grill pan over medium-high heat. Add the scallions, and grill for about 3–5 minutes on each side, until they are charred with dark grill marks. Remove from the heat, roughly chop into small chunks and set aside.

2. Place a dry skillet over low heat and toast the sesame seeds for 5–7 minutes, until golden. Transfer these to a food processor, along with the charred scallions and all the remaining ingredients and blitz until smooth.

Bread & Breakfast

Carrot Cake Cinnamon Buns

I love a cinnamon bun—there's something so comforting about the squidgy dough and all that sweet, buttery, cinnamon filling. Here, I've reinvented it ever so slightly, amplifying it with ginger, walnuts, raisins, and grated carrots to create that warming and familiar spiced carrot cake flavor. I'm also using a Japanese milk bread dough, which is my favorite bread, because it's so fluffy and light thanks to the tangzhong technique for making a quick starter. The tangy, vanilla cream cheese frosting goes hand-in-hand with both carrot cake and cinnamon buns, so it is the perfect finishing touch!

for the tangzhong starter

3 tablespoons (¾oz) strong bread flour
¼ cup (2fl oz) whole milk
¼ cup (2fl oz) water

for the bread dough

2¾ cups (11½oz) strong bread flour
2 tablespoons (½oz) dried milk
  powder
5 tablespoons (2¼oz) superfine sugar
2½ teaspoons (¼oz envelope)
  fast-action dried yeast
1 teaspoon fine sea salt
½ cup (4fl oz) whole milk
1 extra-large egg
4 tablespoons (2¼oz) unsalted butter,
  at room temperature, plus extra for
  greasing

for the carrot filling

⅓ cup (1¾oz) walnuts
¾ stick (6 tablespoons/3oz) unsalted
  butter, room temperature
½ cup (3½oz) superfine sugar
scant ½ cup (3½oz) light soft brown
  sugar
zest of 2 oranges
3 teaspoons ground cinnamon
1 teaspoon ground ginger powder
4 small carrots (5½oz), grated
  (about 1 cup)
⅓ cup (1¾oz) raisins

Continued overleaf >>

1. First make the tangzhong starter. In a small pan, whisk the flour, milk, and water until smooth. Place the pan over medium–low heat and cook, continuously whisking, until the consistency is like custard—when you tilt the pan, it should leave tracks along the bottom. Then transfer to a bowl and set aside to cool.

2. Now make the dough. In the bowl of a stand mixer fitted with a dough hook, combine the flour, milk powder, and sugar, then place the yeast and salt on opposite sides, and mix for a few seconds until just evenly combined.

3. Warm the milk in the microwave for 30 seconds until it reaches around 115°F, then add to the mixer with the egg and cooled starter and knead for 5 minutes on a low speed.

4. Cut the butter into small cubes, then add to the mix in stages, kneading for another 10–12 minutes until the dough is completely smooth and supple. When you stretch it, you should be able to see through it slightly without it breaking.

5. Lightly grease the inside of a large bowl, then shape the dough into a ball and place in the bowl. Cover with plastic wrap and leave in a warm place to rise for 60–90 minutes, until doubled in size.

6. Now make the filling. Place the walnuts on a large, dry pan over low heat and stir for around 10 minutes, until toasted and fragrant, then roughly chop and set aside.

7. In a small bowl, combine the butter, superfine sugar, soft brown sugar and orange zest and beat for about 3 minutes until combined. Add the cinnamon and ginger and mix again.

8. Place the grated carrots in a colander and allow to drain while the dough proofs (they release a lot of moisture). Just before the dough has finished proofing, transfer the carrots to a clean dish towel and squeeze out as much liquid as possible. Then, add them to the butter mixture and mix well to combine.

9. Now it's time to shape the dough. After the dough has doubled in size, punch it down to release any air, then transfer it to a lightly floured worktop.

Continued overleaf >>

for the cream cheese frosting

4 tablespoons (2¼oz) unsalted butter, softened
½ cup (2oz) confectioners' sugar
2 teaspoons vanilla bean paste
a pinch of fine sea salt
¾ cup (6½oz) cream cheese
2 teaspoons honey

TIPS

I recommend using a stand mixer as the dough is quite sticky. However, you can do it by hand; it will just take slightly longer to knead into a smooth dough.

Also, as with all breads, ensure your yeast is in date before baking. I have had too many bread disasters thanks to yeast that is no longer active. Just place your yeast in some warm milk and leave this to stand for a few minutes. It should puff up—if it doesn't, then don't use it!

10. Using a floured rolling pin, roll the dough out into a large rectangle (12 x 17in) and, using a frosting spatula, spread the spiced butter and carrot mixture over the top, then sprinkle over the chopped walnuts and raisins.

11. Starting at one of the short ends, roll the dough up into a tight log. Then, place the palm of your hands on the middle of the log and roll outward to create a longer shape, by an inch.

12. Using a knife, mark out 9 equal portions of dough by making a small indent. Then, take a long length of dental floss and slide this under each indent, then cross over each end of the floss and pull in opposite directions, to cleanly cut through the piece of dough. Repeat until you have 9 pieces. You can use a sharp knife too, but the dental floss gives you much cleaner cuts without affecting the shape.

13. Grease a 16in square baking pan/Dutch oven with butter, then carefully arrange each roll side by side in the dish, leaving a small gap in between. Cover with plastic wrap and let proof in a warm place for 45 minutes until almost doubled in size. At this point, preheat the oven to 350°F/160°C fan/gas mark 4.

14. While the buns are proofing, make the cream cheese frosting. Place the softened butter in a bowl with the confectioners' sugar and beat for about 5 minutes until light and fluffy. Add the vanilla bean paste, salt, and honey, and mix again. Place the cream cheese in a separate large bowl and beat this with a rubber spatula to loosen, then add this to the butter mixture in thirds, folding gently until no streaks remain.

15. Check that the buns have grown in size and are packed tightly in the pan or dish with no gaps in between, then bake for around 25 minutes, until the buns have puffed up and are slightly golden.

16. Leave the buns in the dish to cool down slightly, before slathering over the cream cheese frosting. Pull apart the warm buns and enjoy!

Piña Colada Breakfast Smoothie

I often make a breakfast smoothie with almond milk, but one day we ran out of almond milk and I only had coconut milk. Then I had a lightbulb moment—why not turn my breakfast smoothie into a healthy-ish piña colada? Canned pineapple provides guaranteed sweetness, while lime and mint offset the richness from the coconut and some oats thicken it up. It's fresh, packed full of flavor, and mentally transports me to a tropical paradise. Trust me, it will make your mornings that much more bearable!

12oz canned pineapple (10 rings),
   plus 3½ tablespoons (2fl oz) juice
1¼ cups (10fl oz) cold coconut milk (the drinking
   kind—see My Pantry Ingredients, page 10)
juice of 1 lime
1 teaspoon vanilla bean paste
10 fresh mint leaves
scant ½ cup (1½oz) rolled oats
2 tablespoons honey or agave (VeS)
shredded coconut, to garnish (optional)
fresh pineapple slice, to garnish (optional)

1. Combine all the ingredients in a blender and blitz until smooth.

2. Pour into two glasses, garnish with shredded coconut on top and a slice of fresh pineapple, if you like!

Mum's Turmeric Latte

Turmeric lattes have become trendy recently but my mum has been making them for years, every time I'm run down. It is a warming, comforting, sweet, and slightly spicy drink that will always soothe my throat when I am feeling under the weather. I've found that coconut milk is the best vessel to carry all of the earthy spices, and it provides a natural sweetness and nuttiness that balances it all out perfectly.

3 cardamom pods
5 cloves
½ cinnamon stick
a pinch of ground black pepper
a pinch of ground turmeric
1⅓ cups (11fl oz) coconut milk (the drinking kind—
   see My Pantry Ingredients, page 10)
1in piece of fresh ginger, peeled
2 teaspoons honey or agave (VeS)
coconut whipped cream (optional)
a dusting of ground cinnamon (optional)

1. Place the cardamom, cloves, cinnamon stick, black pepper, and turmeric in a dry pan and stir continuously over low heat for about 5–7 minutes until fragrant.

2. Transfer the spices to a pestle and mortar and grind into a coarse powder.

3. Transfer the spices back to the pan along with the coconut milk and ginger and heat gently for 5 minutes, stirring every so often. You can leave this to infuse for as long as you want.

4. Once you are ready to serve, strain this into a mug and stir through the honey to dissolve. If you want, top with coconut whipped cream and a dusting of cinnamon. Serve hot.

Hazelnut Mocha Monkey Bread

Despite the amount of coffee involved, I first made this bread late at night while my very nocturnal mum was hanging around in the kitchen (and clearing up my mess), watching this creation unfold. It was at about midnight when I turned out the bundt pan to reveal this glossy, insanely aromatic, jewel-topped delight. My mum and I both shouted "WOW"! and devoured about half of it in one sitting. Then my sister came home from a night out and devoured the rest, and I knew it had to be in the book. This one is a slight labor of love, as we'll be making chocolate hazelnut spread stuffed (!) dough balls that each get individually tossed in a coffee-spiked sugar—but I promise you, it is really, really worth it. The hazelnut mocha glaze really marries everything together. Do not leave it out, whatever you do!

for the bread

generous 4 cups (17½oz) strong bread flour, plus extra for dusting

3 tablespoons (1½oz) light soft brown sugar

½ tablespoons (¼oz) fine sea salt

2½ teaspoons (¼oz envelope) fast-action dried yeast

1¼ cups (10fl oz) whole milk

scant 1¾ sticks (6¾oz) unsalted butter (we want to end up with 5¾oz brown butter)

4 teaspoons instant coffee granules

1 egg

for the add-ins

generous 1 cup (5oz) skinned hazelnuts

scant 1 cup (8½oz) chocolate hazelnut spread

1 cup (8oz) light muscovado sugar

2 tablespoons espresso powder

for the hazelnut mocha glaze

1 tablespoon espresso powder

1 tablespoon hot water

2 tablespoons chocolate hazelnut spread

2 tablespoons confectioners' sugar

1 tablespoon whole milk

1. First make the dough. In a large stand mixer bowl, place the flour, sugar, and salt, and stir thoroughly until combined. Make a well in the center and tip in the yeast.

2. Warm the milk in the microwave for about 45 seconds until lukewarm. Pour half into a small pitcher and set aside (this will be our extra liquid that we will add to the dough later).

3. Now we need to brown our butter, so melt it in a pan over low–medium heat, stirring constantly until it starts to bubble up vigorously and a cappuccino-like foam forms at the top. It should smell nutty. At this point, continue stirring for a few more seconds, then turn off the heat and stir again, until you start to see light brown solids form at the bottom. Then transfer the butter immediately to a large bowl, making sure to scrape out all the brown solids from the pan.

4. From the brown butter, take out 2oz (save the rest for the bread assembly) and add this to the first portion of milk and whisk in the coffee. Check that the milk is not too hot, then whisk in the egg too.

5. Pour this wet mixture into the dry ingredients and stir thoroughly to combine, then knead until it forms a soft dough. As needed, add the remaining milk from the second pitcher, continuing to knead for 5 minutes, until the dough is smooth and elastic. If kneading by hand, this will take slightly longer.

6. Transfer the dough to an oiled bowl, cover, and set aside to rise, for 60–90 mins, or until doubled in size.

7. Meanwhile, preheat the oven to 350°F/160°C fan/gas mark 4 and prepare the add-ins. Place the hazelnuts in a large baking pan and toast in the oven for 10 minutes, until golden. Allow to cool slightly, then roughly chop and set aside.

8. Using a pastry bag or a teaspoon, dollop 60 individual teaspoonfuls of chocolate hazelnut spread onto a baking sheet, then place this in the freezer to solidify completely.

Continued overleaf >>

9. Next, make the coffee sugar. In a small bowl, combine the light muscovado sugar with the espresso powder and mix to combine, then set aside.

10. Once the dough has risen, it's time to assemble. Brush a little of the brown butter over the inside of a bundt pan (8½in diameter, 4½in deep). Take your risen dough, which should have doubled in size, and punch it down to release any air. Tip the dough onto a lightly floured counter then portion into 60 pieces (weighing about ½oz each).

11. In a small bowl, combine ⅓ cup (1¼oz) of the chopped toasted hazelnuts with 3 tablespoons of the coffee sugar and 2 tablespoons of brown butter. Mix to combine and then add this at the bottom of the bundt pan.

12. Remove the frozen chocolate hazelnut spread balls from the freezer.

13. Flatten out each piece of dough, place a frozen chocolate hazelnut spread ball in the middle, then fold the dough over until it's completely covered, pinch to seal and roll the dough into a ball. Dunk each ball in the remaining brown butter. Shake off any excess, then toss in the coffee sugar mixture until fully coated. Repeat with all of the dough pieces.

14. Arrange a third of dough balls in the bundt pan, sprinkle over a third of the chopped nuts and repeat this layering process two more times. Once fully assembled, cover lightly with plastic wrap and set aside to proof again for another 45 minutes until nicely puffed up.

15. Finally, bake in the oven for 30–35 minutes until golden.

16. While the bread is baking, make the glaze. In a small bowl, dissolve the espresso in 1 tablespoon hot water. Add the chocolate hazelnut spread and whisk until smooth. Then add the confectioners' sugar and milk and whisk again.

17. Remove the baked bread from the oven. Run a frosting spatula around the edge of the pan and invert the bread onto a large plate and remove the bundt pan. Drizzle liberally with the glaze, then get stuck in, pull apart, and enjoy!

TIP

If you don't have the patience to freeze blobs of chocolate hazelnut spread, I've also tried filling the dough pieces with small chunks of milk chocolate—that works too!

Pumpkin Spice Granola

I am—and always will be—a granola girl. I love having it in the morning with yogurt or cold milk, and it was even my post-clubbing snack for a long time too! So, here I present to you my flavor- and texture-packed granola, flavored with a fan favorite— pumpkin spice! It's so earthy and warming, and reminds me of drinking a sweet and spicy latte in fall. To really capitalize on the pumpkin spice flavor, we have real pumpkin puree going in too for that mellow sweetness, which also acts as a binder for the granola. Chopped dates provide little chewy, toffeelike nuggets, while pecans, cornflakes, pumpkin seeds, and toasted coconut flakes all bring their own level of crunch and flavor.

3 tablespoons (1½fl oz) olive oil

5 tablespoons (2½fl oz) maple syrup

¼ teaspoon fine sea salt

1 teaspoon vanilla bean paste

5 teaspoons ground cinnamon, plus an extra teaspoon, for sprinkling

3 teaspoons ground nutmeg, plus an extra teaspoon, for sprinkling

1 teaspoon ground ginger powder

6 cloves

2¼ cups (9oz) jumbo rolled oats

1¾ cups (1¾oz) cornflakes

⅓ cup (1¾oz) pumpkin seeds

scant ½ cup (1¾oz) pecans

3½oz pitted dates, chopped into small pieces (¾ cup chopped)

½ cup (1½oz) coconut flakes

for the pumpkin puree

1 small butternut squash or pumpkin

olive oil, for drizzling

TIPS

All the spices are toasted to maximize their flavor, and everything is baked low and slow to ensure that it cooks evenly and all the flavors get to know each other.

If you want to use store-bought pumpkin puree (1 cup/8oz), simply ignore the second step.

1. Preheat the oven to 375°F/170°C fan/gas mark 5 or, if you are using ready-made pumpkin puree, preheat to 350°F/160°C fan/gas mark 4.

2. To make your own pumpkin puree, cut the butternut squash or pumpkin lengthwise down the middle. Place flesh-side down on a baking pan, drizzle with oil and then bake it for 35 minutes until the flesh can be mashed easily with a fork and the skin peels away easily. Reduce the oven temperature to 350°F/170°C fan/gas mark 4.

3. Weigh out 8oz roasted squash and add this to a food processor (if using ready-made pumpkin puree, add the same amount to the processor a bowl) along with the olive oil, maple syrup, salt, and vanilla, and blitz until smooth.

4. In a dry skillet, toast the spices, apart from the extra cinnamon and nutmeg, over low heat for 5 minutes until fragrant, then transfer to a pestle and mortar or a spice grinder, and grind into a fine powder. Add the spices to the pumpkin mixture and blitz again to combine.

5. Place the oats, cornflakes, pumpkin seeds, coconut flakes, and pecans in a large baking sheet and mix well to combine. Pour over the pumpkin mixture and, using a rubber spatula, ensure everything is fully coated in the mixture, then flatten down and bake for 1 hour 15 minutes, rotating the pan halfway through.

6. Once baked, this should be golden, crunchy, and formed into one large adhesive granola cluster. Break this into smaller clusters, then sprinkle over 1 teaspoon each of cinnamon and nutmeg and toss to combine. Stir through the dates and toss again.

7. Serve with yogurt or cold milk, or just snack on this on its own, and store the remainder in a large airtight jar.

Tiramisu Pancakes

You know those breakfasts that are so tasty and indulgent that they make you question whether they could double up as a dessert? Well, these tiramisu pancakes fit that brief perfectly! Many of us need a caffeine hit in the morning, so these fluffy, coffee-infused pancakes, studded with chocolate chips for little bursts of sweetness, layered with silky smooth mascarpone cream, and drenched in a coffee maple syrup are just...life-changing. I don't think I can ever eat a normal stack of pancakes again and, whether you make this for breakfast or dessert, make sure you savor every bite.

for the pancakes

4 tablespoons instant coffee granules
2 tablespoons hot water
½ cup (4fl oz) whole milk
1 tablespoon vanilla bean paste
½ teaspoon coffee extract (optional)
1 extra-large egg
2 tablespoons melted unsalted butter (cooled slightly) or olive oil, plus extra for frying
1 cup (4¼oz) self-rising flour
1 teaspoon baking powder
¼ teaspoon fine sea salt
4 tablespoons light soft brown sugar
½ teaspoon apple cider vinegar
¼ cup (1½oz) milk chocolate chips (or more if you want it more chocolatey)
1 tablespoon unsweetened cocoa powder, to dust
¾oz semisweet chocolate, cut into thin shards, to decorate

for the mascarpone

⅔ cup (9oz) mascarpone
2 teaspoons coffee liqueur (optional)
2 tablespoons runny honey
scant ½ cup (3½fl oz) heavy cream
1 tablespoon vanilla bean paste

for the coffee maple syrup

½ teaspoon instant coffee granules
½ tablespoon hot water
4 tablespoons maple syrup

1. First make the pancake batter. In a large bowl, whisk the coffee with the hot water to dissolve, then add the milk, vanilla, and coffee extract and mix again. Add the egg and melted butter and whisk to combine. In a separate bowl, combine the flour, baking powder, salt, and sugar, and mix to combine. Make a well in the center and slowly pour in the wet mixture, whisking the batter constantly until there are no lumps. Add in the vinegar and mix to combine, then set aside at room temperature for about 15 minutes.

2. To make the mascarpone cream, in a bowl, combine the mascarpone, coffee liqueur, honey, and vanilla, and mix until smooth. In a separate bowl, whisk the heavy cream to soft peaks, making sure not to overwhisk. Using a rubber spatula, gently fold this into the mascarpone and place in the refrigerator until ready to assemble.

3. For the coffee maple syrup, combine the coffee granules with ½ tablespoon hot water in a small pan and stir until dissolved. Add the maple syrup and place over low heat, stirring constantly, until slightly thickened. Remove from the heat and pour into a small dish.

4. Now it's time to fry the pancakes! Place a large nonstick skillet over medium–low heat and melt 1 tablespoon butter. Once the pan is warm, spoon three large circles of batter onto each corner of the pan. Sprinkle chocolate chips over each pancake (about 10 chips per pancake) and cook for 2½ minutes—bubbles should form on top. Carefully flip the pancakes and cook for another 2 minutes, then transfer to a plate and keep warm. Repeat this process with the rest of the batter, topping up the pan with more butter if needed when frying.

5. Now, you're ready to see this masterpiece come together. Place one pancake on a plate and spread 1 heaping tablespoon of the mascarpone cream on top. Repeat this stack-and-spread process with the pancakes, until you have a tall stack, with the top layer being mascarpone cream.

6. Using a small sifter, dust the stack with cocoa powder, and sprinkle with your wonderfully thin chocolate shards. You can either drench the entire stack or each individual pancake in coffee maple syrup and then of course tuck in immediately.

Miso, Peanut & Date Banana Bread

Banana bread is a household favorite for many, so I did feel hesitant about revamping it. Do not fret, however, as this still tastes like a recognizable banana bread, but with a richer, more balanced flavor profile. We've got brown butter and olive oil to create lovely, nutty undertones, and the miso adds that characteristic umami flavor, which perfectly balances out the sweetness of the bananas. The dates turn into little chewy nuggets that taste like toffee and contrast with the salty peanut crunch. As everyone knows, banana bread is best served with butter and this whipped miso brown butter just makes every single flavor sing.

for the banana bread

½ cup (4¼oz) unsalted butter (about 3½oz once browned)

4 tablespoons (2¾oz) white or red miso paste

2 tablespoons (1fl oz) olive oil

1 tablespoon vanilla bean paste

2½ tablespoons (1oz) superfine sugar

3½ tablespoons (1¾oz) dark soft brown sugar

2½ tablespoons (1¼oz) light soft brown sugar

1¾ cups (7½oz) all-purpose flour

1 teaspoon baking powder

1 teaspoon ground cinnamon

scant ½ cup (1¾oz) chopped roasted salted peanuts

⅓ cup (1¾oz) pitted dates, chopped

1 extra-large egg

2 large ripe bananas (9oz)

2 tablespoons turbinado sugar

for the whipped miso brown butter

5½ tablespoons (2¾oz) unsalted butter, to brown

3½ tablespoons (1¾oz) unsalted butter, at room temperature

1 teaspoon red or white miso paste

3 teaspoons maple syrup

TIP

If you have any leftover banana bread the following day, toast or broil slices of banana bread and then spread over the butter for an even better eating experience!

1. Preheat the oven to 350°F/160°C fan/gas mark 4 and line a 8½in x 4½in x 2½in loaf pan with parchment paper.

2. First, brown all the butter—for the banana bread and whipped miso brown butter. Place 1¾ sticks (7oz) butter in a large pan over low heat and stir constantly until you see it bubble up vigorously with a thick, cappuccino-like foam, and light brown solids start to form at the bottom. At this point, take the pan off the heat, stirring for about 30 more seconds, then immediately transfer it to a bowl, making sure to scrape out all the solids from the bottom, as these carry so much flavor. Weigh 3½oz from what you have into another bowl and put the rest in the refrigerator for making the miso brown butter.

3. To the bowl with the warm brown butter, add the miso paste and olive oil and whisk until combined. Add the vanilla bean paste, along with all the sugars and whisk again until combined. The mixture may still be warm, so set aside to cool while you prepare the dry ingredients.

4. In a separate bowl, combine the flour, baking powder and cinnamon. Remove about 2 tablespoons and transfer to a small bowl. To this add the chopped peanuts and dates and mix to coat in the flour. This will prevent them from sinking.

5. Add the egg to the cooled wet mixture, whisking well until homogeneous. In a separate bowl, mash the bananas with a fork or potato masher, until as smooth as possible, then add this to the wet mixture and mix to combine.

6. Using a rubber spatula, fold the dry mixture into the wet mixture in three parts, until no flour pockets remain. Finally, fold in the dates and peanuts until well dispersed. Transfer the batter to the lined pan, sprinkle with turbinado sugar, and bake for 55 minutes–1 hour, until a skewer comes out clean.

7. While the bread is baking, finish the whipped butter. Mix the room temperature butter with the miso paste until thoroughly combined. Add the reserved, chilled brown butter and whisk, then add the maple syrup and whisk again until smooth.

8. To serve, remove the baked banana bread from the pan and cool on a cooling rack. Then slice it up and slather on the whipped butter.

Cookies & Sweet Treats

Maple, Pecan & Apple Popcorn Bites

This is one of the easiest recipes in the book, and my homage to the gooey marshmallow and crispy rice bars I used to love as a kid. Here, I've added popcorn for extra crunch and taken the flavors one step further with my favorite combination of apples, pecans, maple, and brown butter. We're using dried apples, which have a lovely, concentrated flavor and a chewy texture to contrast against the crispy elements, with buttery roasted pecans and nutty brown butter that pair perfectly with the mellow maple syrup. When I first made these, my family devoured the entire pan in one day, which is hopefully a testament to how addictive they are!

1 cup (4oz) pecans
10 cups (2½oz) salted popped popcorn/⅔ cup (4oz) popcorn kernels (if popping from scratch)
2¾ cups (2¾oz)puffed rice cereal
½ cup (4oz) dried apple rings, roughly chopped
8 tablespoons (4oz) unsalted butter
5 tablespoons (2½fl oz) maple syrup
1 teaspoon vanilla bean paste
½ teaspoon fine sea salt
8½oz white marshmallows

for the maple glaze

2 tablespoons (½oz) confectioners' sugar
1 teaspoon vanilla bean paste
1 tablespoon maple syrup
a pinch of fine sea salt

1. Preheat the oven to 350°F/160°C fan/gas mark 4 and line an 8in square dish with parchment paper.

2. Arrange the pecans on a baking sheet and roast for 10 minutes in the oven, then allow to cool slightly before chopping into small chunks. Set aside.

3. If making popcorn from scratch, pop the popcorn either in the microwave or in a dry pan on the stove, discarding any unpopped kernels.

4. In a large bowl, combine the popcorn with the pecans, puffed rice cereal, and chopped apples and mix to combine.

5. Place the butter in a large pan (this needs to be deep and wide as it will double up as our mixing bowl), and melt over low heat, stirring continuously for about 10 minutes. You want to take it past the point of melting until it froths vigorously and you start to see light brown solids form at the bottom. At this point, immediately add the maple syrup, vanilla bean paste and salt and stir to combine.

6. Then, add in the marshmallows and stir until the mixture is melted and smooth. Remove from the heat.

7. Pour the dry popcorn mixture into the marshmallow mixture, and use a rubber spatula to mix really well, ensuring everything is coated in the marshmallow mixture.

8. Tip the mixture into the prepared dish and press down firmly to make sure it is as compact as possible (I like to splash my hands with a bit of water to make it easier to handle). Transfer to the refrigerator to firm up.

9. Now make the glaze. Combine everything in a small bowl and whisk well until smooth. Drizzle this liberally over the popcorn mix, then place back in the refrigerator to firm up for at least 2 hours. Cut into 16 squares.

"Pecans have a wonderful depth of flavor—so buttery and sweet. Once they're roasted, their aroma envelops you like a cozy, fall hug."

MAKES 12 | PREP: 15 MINS | BAKE: 25 MINS | VG

Coconut & Yuzu Shortbread

Yuzu has a wonderful, refreshing citrus flavor that I like to think of as a cross between a lemon, grapefruit, and clementine. The yuzu fruit itself is not readily available, so I always use bottled yuzu juice, which works wonderfully. A little goes a long way in this recipe, as we just need a small amount to create a punchy glaze. The sharpness provides a lovely contrast to the buttery nuttiness of the coconut and brings just the right amount of citrus sweetness, resulting in a perfectly balanced cookie with a unique—yet somewhat familiar—flavor. Teatime will never be the same again once you've tried these!

generous 1 cup (3½oz) shredded coconut

scant 1½ sticks (¾ cup/5½oz) unsalted butter, at room temperature

⅔ cup (2½oz) confectioners' sugar

1 teaspoon vanilla bean paste

1 teaspoon coconut extract (optional)

½ teaspoon fine sea salt

1 egg yolk

2¼ cups (9½oz) all-purpose flour, plus extra for dusting

for the frosting

scant 1 cup (3½oz) confectioners' sugar

2 tablespoons yuzu juice

1. Preheat the oven to 350°F/160°C fan/gas mark 4 and line a baking sheet with parchment paper.

2. Place the coconut in a large, dry skillet over medium heat and toast for about 5–7 minutes, stirring constantly, until it turns a light golden brown. Remove from the heat and transfer to a bowl to cool down.

3. In a large bowl, cream together the butter, confectioners' sugar, vanilla, coconut extract (if using) and salt until combined. This can be done in a stand mixer with a paddle attachment, or simply with a wooden spoon. Beat in the egg yolk, then add a scant cup (1¾oz) of the toasted coconut (reserving ¼ cup/¾oz) for decoration) and mix again. Finally, gently fold in the flour until just combined, making sure not to overmix.

4. Tip the dough onto a floured worktop and gently roll out into a 8½in circle, about ¾in thick. Cut this into quarters, then cut each quarter into 3 triangles, so you end up with 12. Arrange these on the baking sheet.

5. Bake the cookies in the oven for around 25 minutes, rotating the sheet halfway through, until golden. Allow to cool on the sheet (they will be very delicate once baked) before transferring to a wire rack to cool completely.

6. While the cookies are cooling down, make the frosting. Place the confectioners' sugar in a shallow bowl and whisk in the yuzu juice until there are no lumps.

7. Dip the top surface of each (cooled) cookie into the frosting. Quickly shake off the excess, then place them back on the cooling rack, dry-side down. Sprinkle the frosting with the remaining toasted coconut, then allow the frosting to dry for about 30 minutes before tucking in!

TIPS

Make sure you use yuzu juice and NOT an extract, as they have completely different flavors. See My Pantry Ingredients on page 10 for more information.

As with any shortbread recipe, please do not overmix the dough, as you risk losing the crumbly, short texture.

Cookies & Sweet Treats

Baklava-inspired Flapjacks

Now, baklava is my favorite sweet treat of all time. The combination of nuts and syrup with the hints of spices just hits every spot for me. So, here I'm taking the nutty and fragrant elements of baklava to revamp the humble (but also sticky and perfectly indulgent) flapjack. If you don't like rose water, orange works really well too, and you can even grate some orange zest and add it to the nutty filling. And yes, I know sesame seeds are not found in baklava, but I love the nuttiness and crunch that they bring. To me, this is perfection!

for the nut filling

5½ tablespoons (2¾oz) unsalted butter, melted
¾ cup (3½oz) pistachios
¾ cup (3½oz) walnuts
3½ tablespoons (1½oz) superfine sugar
2½ teaspoons ground cinnamon
1½ tablespoons (¾oz) honey

for the flapjacks

5 tablespoons sesame seeds
3½ cups (12oz) rolled oats
2 sticks (1 cup/7½oz) unsalted butter
¼ cup (2¼oz) light soft brown sugar
3 tablespoons (2¼oz) corn syrup
3 tablespoons (2¼oz) honey
¼ teaspoon fine sea salt
1½ teaspoons cinnamon
3 teaspoons rose water

for the glaze

8 tablespoons (5½oz) honey
juice of 1 lemon
6 teaspoons rose water
1 teaspoon rose petals, to decorate
1 teaspoon crushed pistachios, to decorate

TIPS

Cold flapjacks are easier to slice, so I store these in the refrigerator. Warm flapjacks tend to crumble.

To make this vegan, swap the honey for more corn syrup and use vegan butter in place of regular butter.

1. Preheat the oven to 375°F/170°C fan/gas mark 5 and line an 8in square baking pan with parchment paper.

2. First make the nut filling. Place 2 tablespoons of the melted butter in a large bowl with the pistachios and walnuts and toss to coat. Transfer the nuts to a baking sheet and roast these for 10 minutes until lightly golden and fragrant. Once roasted and cooled, very finely chop half of these (a food processor works best), and then chop the rest into small chunks (we want them to have some bite). Place all the nuts in a bowl and mix these together with the superfine sugar and cinnamon. Then, stir the honey into the remaining melted butter until smooth and pour this over the nut mixture. Stir until well combined and set aside while you make the flapjack batter.

3. In a large dry skillet, toast the sesame seeds over low heat for about 5 minutes until golden and fragrant, then transfer to a bowl with the oats and mix together.

4. In a large pan over a low-medium heat, place the butter, sugar, corn syrup, honey, salt, and cinnamon and melt, stirring, until everything is combined. Turn off the heat and stir through the rose water, then gradually add the oat mixture and mix well.

5. Pour half of this into the baking pan and flatten down with a rubber spatula, then spread the nut mixture in a layer on top, again flattening out with a rubber spatula. Finally, spread the rest of the flapjack batter over the nuts and press down well until flat. Transfer to the oven and bake for around 25 minutes until firm and slightly browned around the edges.

6. Meanwhile, make the glaze. In a small bowl, mix together the honey, lemon juice and rose water. Once the flapjacks are baked, brush this glaze all over the top. Allow the flapjacks to cool completely; first at room temperature, and then in the refrigerator for at least 2 hours, until completely cold.

7. Turn out of the pan and cut the flapjacks into diamond-shaped pieces (like baklava)—first slicing vertically in ¾in strips, and then slicing diagonally across. Decorate with pistachios and rose petals if you like.

Miso Tahini Oat Cookies

I always want more salty, umami, and nutty flavors from a bog-standard chocolate chip cookie, and I also want it to be chewy, yet slightly crispy around the edges. These cookies deliver on all fronts. To balance out the saltiness from miso, we've got white chocolate chips, as well as tahini for that added nuttiness and sesame for crunch. The oats also provide extra texture, and the brown butter creates that lovely, mellow, nutty flavor, which marries everything together. This recipe makes a lot of cookies, which is intentional because they will all vanish before you can even blink! I could suggest that you halve the recipe, but really, I wouldn't bother.

scant ½ cup (3½oz) unsalted butter (this will be browned so we should end up with 2¾oz)
1½ cups (6¾oz) all-purpose flour
1 cup plus 2 tablespoons (4½oz) jumbo oats, divided in method
½ teaspoon baking soda
½ teaspoon baking powder
2½ tablespoons (1¼oz) extra virgin coconut oil
3 tablespoons (3oz) white miso paste
⅓ cup (2¾oz) white tahini
2 teaspoons vanilla bean paste
1 cup (8½oz) light soft brown sugar
¼ cup plus 2 tablespoons (2¾oz) superfine sugar
1 extra-large egg
scant 1 cup (5½oz) white chocolate chips (I like a mixture of chocolate chips and chocolate chunks)
2½ tablespoons (1½oz) white sesame seeds
2½ tablespoons (1½oz) black sesame seeds

TIP

You can chill the cookie dough in the refrigerator overnight, and then scoop into balls and bake immediately the next day. The cookie dough balls can also be frozen and baked straight from frozen for 20 minutes.

1. Melt the butter in a large pan over medium–low heat, stirring continuously for about 10 minutes. Once it froths vigorously and you start to see light brown solids form at the bottom immediately take it off the heat, stirring continuously for a few more seconds, then transfer to a bowl to stop it from burning and use a rubber spatula to scrape out all the brown solids. After this process, weigh the butter again and top off with regular butter if necessary, so you have 2¾oz. Set aside to cool.

2. In a separate bowl, combine the flour, 1 cup (4oz) jumbo oats, baking soda, and baking powder.

3. Add the coconut oil to the brown butter and whisk to combine, then add the white miso, whisking until homogeneous, then the tahini, vanilla bean paste and both sugars and whisk well. Making sure the batter is cool to the touch, beat in the egg until smooth.

4. Using a rubber spatula, fold the dry ingredients into the wet batter until just combined, then stir through the white chocolate chips and chunks. Cover the bowl in plastic wrap and refrigerate for 1 hour, to firm up.

5. While the dough is chilling, toast the white and black sesame seeds in a dry skillet over low heat for about 7 minutes. Transfer to a bowl and mix with 2 tablespoons jumbo oats.

6. Once the dough has chilled, divide into 32 portions, about 1¼oz each (or use an ice-cream scoop, if easier) and use your hands to roll these into balls. Toss each ball in the bowl of sesame and oats until coated before placing on a baking sheet.

7. Chill all the dough balls in the refrigerator for 1 hour to firm up, then, 10 minutes before the time is up, preheat the oven to 350°F/160°C fan/gas mark 4.

8. Arrange about 8 dough balls on a lined baking sheet, well-spaced as they will spread, and bake the cookies for around 15 minutes, rotating the sheet halfway through, until golden. Repeat with the remaining dough, then allow to cool on the sheet first, before transferring to a cooling rack to cool completely.

Blonde Chocolate Rocky Roads

Rocky Roads were the first sweet treat I learned how to make when I was younger, and I was in awe—the flavor sensations in each bite, in addition to the different textures, really astounded me. So, my reinvented recipe still has a variety of textures, but uses cornflakes and roasted almonds with spiced speculoos cookies for crunch and floral-scented apricots for a contrasting chewy texture. Caramelized white chocolate is the star of the show. It's a slight labor of love but, I promise you, it is worth it. By roasting the white chocolate, you caramelize the sugars and the result is a mellow, caramel-flavored chocolate. When caramelizing your white chocolate, you want to use a really good-quality one with a high content of cocoa solids (ideally 32 percent).

9oz white chocolate, broken into small pieces
⅔ cup (2¾oz) almonds
1 cup (2¾oz) broken spiced speculoos cookies (break into small chunks)
2¼ cups (2¼oz) cornflakes
⅓ cup (2¾oz) dried apricots (dried cranberries work really well here too), roughly chopped
¼ teaspoon fine sea salt

1. Preheat the oven to 275°F/120°C fan/gas mark 1.

2. Arrange the white chocolate on a roasting pan and roast in the oven for 1½ hours—every 10 minutes, take out the pan and mix and smooth down the chocolate. It may seem chalky at first but the more you mix it, the more it will smooth out. Once the chocolate has caramelized and resembles a smooth, golden, melted chocolate, transfer it to a large mixing bowl and turn the oven up to 350°F/160°C fan/gas mark 4.

3. Place the almonds on a roasting pan and roast for 10 minutes, then allow to cool slightly before roughly chopping—ensure they are still chunky. Add these to the melted chocolate along with the spiced speculoos, cornflakes, and dried apricots.

4. Add the salt and give everything a good mix to ensure it is well combined, then pour into a 8in square container and refrigerate for 2 hours, or until set. Cut into 24 small squares and enjoy.

TIP

You can now buy slabs of caramelized chocolate, often called "blonde" chocolate, so feel free to use that if you are short on time.

Pecan Pie Skillet Cookie

Pecan pie and skillet cookies are two iconic, sharing desserts that remind me of family get-togethers when I was a kid, so naturally I've combined the two. The trick here is to partially bake the cookie dough first in a cast-iron skillet, then make a slight well in the center and pour in that gooey pecan filling, then put this back in the oven to bake, so you end up with two distinctive textures.

for the cookie

scant 1 cup (3½oz) pecans
2¼ sticks (8¼ cups/9oz) unsalted butter (we will be browning this so should end up with 8½oz)
scant 1 cup (7oz) soft light brown sugar
½ cup (4oz) superfine sugar
2 extra-large eggs
2 teaspoons vanilla bean paste
scant 3 cups (12oz) all-purpose flour
1½ teaspoons baking powder
1 teaspoon baking soda
1 teaspoon fine sea salt
3½oz milk chocolate, chopped into small pieces

for the pecan pie topping

scant 1 cup (3½oz) pecans
5 tablespoons (2½oz) unsalted butter (this will be browned so we should end up with 2¼oz)
5 tablespoons (2½oz) soft light brown sugar
⅓ cup (3oz) maple syrup
3 tablespoons (1¾oz) corn syrup
2 extra-large eggs
2 teaspoons vanilla bean paste
1 tablespoon flour
¼ teaspoon fine sea salt

1. Preheat the oven to 350°F/160°C fan/gas mark 4.

2. First roast all the pecans (2¾ cup/7oz) that you will be using both for the cookies and the topping. Place them in a baking pan and roast in the oven for 10 minutes, until toasted and fragrant. Divide in two; set aside half for the topping, and chop the remaining pecans into small chunks, but not too fine.

3. Next, brown the butter, for both the cookie and the topping. Melt scant 3 sticks (1½ cups/11¾oz) butter in a large pan over low heat, stirring continuously for about 10 minutes. Once it froths vigorously and light brown solids form at the bottom, immediately take it off the heat, stirring continuously for a few more seconds, then transfer to a bowl to stop it from burning and use a rubber spatula to scrape out all the brown solids. After this process, weigh out 2¼oz and set aside for later, then weigh out the remainder, which should be 8½oz. If it's less, top it up with regular butter.

4. To make the cookie, whisk the sugars into the 8½oz brown butter, then allow to cool for a few minutes. Beat in the eggs, one by one then mix in the vanilla bean paste until combined.

5. In a separate bowl, whisk the flour, baking powder, baking soda and salt until combined. Fold these dry ingredients into the wet batter, then fold through the chocolate and chopped pecans until well dispersed through the dough.

6. Transfer the dough to a skillet and press down firmly, then bake in the oven for 20 minutes while you make the topping.

7. Add the brown sugar to the reserved 2¼oz brown butter and whisk to combine. Add both syrups and whisk again. Add the eggs, one by one, and whisk until homogeneous, then whisk in the vanilla bean paste. Add the flour and salt and mix to combine.

8. After 20 minutes, remove the skillet from the oven. Using a rubber spatula, press down the middle of the cookie, leaving a ¾in border around the edge. Arrange the reserved whole pecans in the center, in a circular pattern, until no gaps remain, then carefully pour in the topping (if some flows onto the border, that's okay).

9. Place the skillet back in the oven and bake for another 25–30 minutes, until the crust is golden, with a slight wobble in the center. Serve as a warm, gooey cookie, with ice cream on the side, or chill it in the refrigerator for 3–8 hours or overnight to harden before slicing.

Ginger, Coconut, & Dark Chocolate Oat Cookies

I love the classic oaty cookie, but I also love a ginger snap, so here I've created a hybrid of the two—oaty, crunchy, and comforting, but with a really warming and fiery ginger flavor. The ginger is offset with toasted coconut, which brings a lovely, nutty flavor to complement the oats. They are then dipped in bitter, semisweet chocolate, which just marries everything together. This is definitely one of my (and my dad's) favorite flavor combinations and these are perfect with a cup of hot tea.

1½ cups (4½oz) shredded coconut, divided in method

1⅓ cups (5½oz) all-purpose flour

1 teaspoon baking powder

½ teaspoon baking soda

4 teaspoons ground ginger powder

¼ teaspoon fine sea salt

¾ cup (2½oz) rolled oats

scant 1½ sticks (¾ cup/5½oz) unsalted butter, at room temperature

generous ¾ cup (5½oz) golden superfine sugar (or regular superfine sugar)

1 teaspoon vanilla bean paste

2 tablespoons corn syrup

1 tablespoon stem ginger syrup

6 bulbs of stem ginger (3½oz), finely diced (2 tablespoons)

4½oz semisweet chocolate

1 tablespoon (½oz) coconut oil

1. Preheat the oven to 350°F/160°C fan/gas mark 4.

2. Place the shredded coconut in a dry skillet over medium–low heat and toast, stirring, for 5–7 minutes until golden. Transfer to a dish and set aside.

3. In a large bowl, combine the flour, baking powder, baking soda, ground ginger, salt, and oats with ⅔ cup (2oz) of the toasted coconut and mix well to combine. Set aside.

4. In a separate bowl, beat together the butter and sugar until well combined. You can do this in a stand mixer with a paddle attachment or by hand with a wooden spoon. Add the vanilla and beat again, then add both syrups and beat to incorporate.

5. Next, fold the dry ingredients into the wet batter, until no flour pockets remain. Finally, add the stem ginger and mix until dispersed through the dough.

6. Divide the dough into ¾oz portions and roll these into balls—you should end up with 26 in total. Place ½ cup (1½oz) of the toasted coconut in a large bowl and roll each ball in the coconut until coated, then place about 8 balls on a lined baking sheet (spaced out as the cookies will spread).

7. Bake in the oven for 20–25 minutes until golden and crisp, rotating the sheet halfway through, and let cool on the baking sheet before transferring to a wire rack to cool completely and harden. Repeat the baking process with the remaining dough balls.

8. Once the cookies are completely cool, melt the semisweet chocolate with the coconut oil in a shallow, heatproof bowl in the microwave in 10-second increments until smooth.

9. Dip the flat side of each cookie in the chocolate, shake off the excess, then place these back on the wire rack, chocolate side facing up. Sprinkle the remaining coconut over the chocolate and, once all coated, place the cookies in the refrigerator for a final 5 minutes to harden, then enjoy.

TIP

Replace the butter with vegan butter to make these 100% vegan.

Pistachio, White Chocolate & Cardamom Millionaire Shortbread

This one reminds me of being a kid at the supermarket, eyeing up all the freshly made treats in the bakery aisle. Millionaire shortbread always caught my eye, because of all of those fascinating layers, so here I've simply put all of my favorite flavors—brown butter, cardamom, and pistachio—inside to create a nutty, spiced, and slightly sweet treat. I've swapped milk chocolate for white chocolate, as I think it pairs really well with the cardamom. However, I've gone for a white chocolate ganache over plain white chocolate, so that it's not sickly sweet alongside the caramel. Making caramel can often be somewhat intimidating, but I've included a few tips and tricks that should help you breeze through it!

for the shortbread dough
⅓ cup (1¾oz) pistachios

1½ sticks (¾ cup/6oz) unsalted butter, cubed (this will be browned so should end up with ⅔ cup/5½oz)

21 cardamom pods (which gives 2 teaspoons ground powder)

¼ teaspoon fine sea salt

½ cup (2½oz) cornstarch

⅔ cup (2½oz) all-purpose flour

6 tablespoons (1½oz) whole wheat spelt flour

⅔ cup (2½oz) confectioners' sugar

1 teaspoon vanilla bean paste

for the caramel
1 stick (½ cup/4oz) unsalted butter, cubed

½ cup (4fl oz) heavy cream

1 cup (7oz) superfine sugar

1 tablespoon liquid glucose (optional, but recommended as this helps prevent crystallization when making caramel)

½ teaspoon fine sea salt

⅓ cup (1¾oz) roasted pistachios

2 tablespoons pistachio cream (optional)

Continued overleaf >>

1. First, roast all of the pistachios that are needed for all three layers (1 cup/4¾oz) on a large baking pan and roast these for 10 minutes. Remove, and use a pestle and mortar (or a food processor) to break these into smaller pieces (but not too fine, as we want them chunky). Set aside.

2. Melt the 1½ sticks (6oz) butter in a large pan over medium–low heat, stirring continuously for about 10 minutes. Take it past the point of melting until it froths vigorously and you start to see light brown solids form at the bottom. Immediately take it off the heat, stirring continuously for a few more seconds, then transfer to a bowl to stop it from burning and use a rubber spatula to scrape out all the brown solids, which carry so much flavor. After this, weigh the butter again and top off with regular butter if necessary, so you have 5½oz. Set aside to cool.

3. Place the cardamom pods in a large, dry skillet over low heat and toast, stirring, for about 10 minutes until fragrant. Transfer to a pestle and mortar, bash to release the seeds from the shells, then grind the seeds to a fine powder and discard the shells (I store my shells in a tub and add them to my chai), or blitz everything, including the shells, in a spice grinder.

4. In a large bowl (or food processor), combine the ground cardamom, salt, cornstarch, flours, and confectioners' sugar and whisk or pulse well to combine. Add ⅓ cup (1¾oz) of the chopped pistachios and mix again to combine.

5. Stir the vanilla into the cooled brown butter, then slowly add this to the dry ingredients in a steady stream and mix until it forms a dough, making sure not to overmix. As soon as you have a cohesive dough, quickly press it into a lined 8in square baking pan, flattening it down using the bottom of a jar or mug. Chill in the refrigerator for 10 minutes to firm up. Meanwhile preheat the oven to 350°F/160°C fan/gas mark 4. Once cooled, bake the shortbread dough in the oven for 25 minutes.

Continued overleaf >>

for the white chocolate ganache

6½oz white chocolate, finely chopped

¼ cup (2fl oz) heavy cream

2–3 tablespoons (¾oz) chopped pistachios, to decorate

TIP

> The addition of spelt flour in the shortbread adds a lovely nuttiness to complement the brown butter in the dough. However, you can just use all-purpose flour instead if you can't get your hands on any.

6. Once baked, place on a wire rack to cool down completely, still in the pan, until firm.

7. While the cookie is baking, make the caramel. In a small pan, gently heat the butter and cream over very low heat, stirring to mix, until steaming but not boiling.

8. In a separate heavy pan (make sure that this is not a nonstick pan), use a clean spoon to mix together the sugar and liquid glucose with 3½ tablespoons (1½fl oz) water. Make sure the sugar is submerged in the water, then place over low heat until dissolved. Once dissolved, increase the heat and boil rapidly until the syrup turns a brown caramel color—do not stir.

9. Once this has turned into a caramel, remove the pan from the heat and carefully pour the cream mixture into the caramel pan, whisking constantly. Be careful as this may splatter. Place this back on the heat and continue to whisk until the sauce reaches 244 F on a candy thermometer (which should take about 1 minute). Once ready, stir through the salt, and transfer the caramel to a bowl to cool down slightly, and then stir through ½ cup (1¾oz) of the chopped pistachios.

10. Once the cookie is cool to the touch, pour the caramel over the top and smooth it down. If you like, at this point you can also swirl the pistachio cream through the caramel. Transfer to the refrigerator to chill and set for 45 minutes–1 hour.

11. When the caramel has almost finished setting, start making the white chocolate ganache. Place the chocolate in a bowl and gently heat the heavy cream in a pan until steaming, but not boiling.

12. Once the cream is hot, pour this over the white chocolate. Leave it to stand for 30 seconds, and then slowly stir with a rubber spatula, starting from the inside in a circular motion, until the white chocolate and the cream are combined and homogeneous.

13. Remove the set caramel from the refrigerator and pour over the white chocolate ganache. Use a frosting or offset spatula to spread it out evenly. Sprinkle over the remaining pistachios and then place it back in the refrigerator to set for 10 minutes.

14. This shortbread is very decadent and rich, so I find that it is best served as bite-size squares. I recommend cutting it into 36 mini pieces, before tucking in!

Pecan, Coconut & Caramel Brownies

I'm (somewhat controversially) not a huge fan of chocolate cake, or very chocolatey things, but I do love German chocolate cake. It's layered with this incredible gooey filling, with an abundance of coconut, pecans, and a caramel-type sauce made from evaporated milk, which reminds me of dulce de leche. So I've transported all of these delicious flavors to a pan of brownies. We've got brown butter and a hint of coffee in the batter, which you can hardly taste but they really amplify the chocolate flavor and they marry beautifully with the buttery pecans and coconut.

for the caramel filling

1 x 14oz can condensed milk (or buy dulce de leche if you want to save time)
1⅓ cups (5¼oz) pecans, divided in method
1 cup plus 2 tablespoons (3½oz) toasted coconut flakes, divided in method
1 teaspoon vanilla bean paste
½ teaspoon fine sea salt
1 egg

for the brownie batter

3½oz semisweet chocolate
6½oz milk chocolate, divided in method
1¾ sticks (7oz) unsalted butter
3 extra-large eggs
½ cup (3½oz) golden superfine sugar
⅔ cup (5¼oz) light brown soft sugar
1 tablespoon instant coffee
1 tablespoon hot water
scant 1 cup (4oz) all-purpose flour
3 tablespoons (¾oz) unsweetened cocoa powder
½ teaspoon fine sea salt
½ teaspoon sea salt flakes, for sprinkling

1. First prepare the caramel filling, which means making the dulce de leche from the can of condensed milk (you can even do this the night before). Remove the labels from the unopened can and place it in a large pan filled with water—it should be completely submerged. Cover tightly with a lid and boil for at least 4 hours—you want a really strong color on your dulce de leche. Check the pan every so often to ensure that the water is not evaporating and top off if necessary. After 4 hours, switch off the heat and use tongs to carefully remove the can from the hot water, and allow this to cool before using. If you boil this for a shorter amount of time, the dulce de leche will be lighter, and the flavor will not be as strong. Alternatively, you can use store-bought dulce de leche.

2. Preheat the oven to 350°F/160°C fan/gas mark 4, then roast the pecans in a baking pan for 15 minutes until toasted and golden. Allow to cool slightly before roughly chopping into small chunks. (If your coconut flakes weren't pretoasted, you can add these to the pan with the pecans and roast them at the same time.)

3. Pour the cooled dulce de leche into a bowl and whisk to loosen. Add the vanilla bean paste and salt and whisk to combine. Ensuring the mixture is cool, beat in the egg and whisk until homogeneous.

4. To this mixture add in 1 cup (4oz) chopped pecans and 1 cup (3oz) toasted coconut flakes (reserving the rest for later), mix well to combine, then set aside while you make the brownie batter.

5. Break all of the semisweet chocolate and 3oz of the milk chocolate into pieces in a large heatproof bowl. Next, we're going to brown the butter. Place the butter in a large pan over low heat, stirring continuously for about 10 minutes. You want to take it past the point of melting until it froths vigorously and you start to see light brown solids form at the bottom. Immediately take it off the heat and pour it into a bowl and weigh it out again—it should be 6½oz but top off with more butter if needed. Then pour it over the chocolate, using a rubber spatula to scrape out all the brown solids, which carry so much flavor. Leave the chocolate to stand for 30 seconds, then slowly mix the mixture together, until smooth and homogeneous.

Continued overleaf >>

6. In the bowl of a stand mixer with a whisk attachment, mix the eggs and both sugars. Whisk on high for around 7 minutes (longer or shorter depending on the power of your mixer) until the batter is pale and has doubled in size. The mixture should leave a trail for a few seconds when drizzled on itself.

7. Using a rubber spatula, carefully fold the chocolate mixture into the batter, until no streaks remain. Dissolve the instant coffee in the hot water, then fold this in too.

8. In a separate bowl, whisk together the flour, cocoa powder and fine sea salt. Remove 1 tablespoon of this and add this to a bowl. Chop the remaining 3½oz milk chocolate into small chunks, then add these to the small bowl with flour and toss until coated. This is to prevent them from sinking.

9. Sift in the flour mixture to the wet batter in three parts, folding gently each time until no flour pockets remain. Finally, fold through the chocolate chunks until evenly distributed.

10.Pour the batter into a deep 8in square pan lined with parchment paper and level with a rubber spatula or frosting spatula. Now dollop spoonfuls of the dulce de leche mixture all over the top of the batter, then swirl this into the batter using a butter knife or skewer. Finally, sprinkle with the remaining pecans and the 2 tablespoons toasted coconut, with a few sea salt flakes.

11. Bake in the oven for 35–40 minutes, until firm around the edges with a slight wobble in the center. Let cool completely in the pan, then transfer to the refrigerator to chill and harden for at least 4 hours, or overnight. Slice into 16 squares, or 24 smaller squares if serving as a smaller treat.

TIPS

The key to brownies is to underbake them slightly as they will continue to cook in the residual heat of the pan, and then you MUST let them chill and harden completely before eating, to really appreciate the flavors and textures.

I recommend a stand mixer for this recipe, because we want to whip a significant amount of air into the eggs - this is what will give the brownies their characteristic "crackled" top.

Tahini, Peanut & White Chocolate Blondies

I have a bit of a blondie obsession—I can't get enough of that fudgy texture with those mellow, caramel flavors! This recipe, with brown butter, tahini, and roasted peanuts, off-set with chunks of white chocolate, is a sweet and slightly salty dream. Luckily, they are extremely easy to make (even easier than brownies). With no need for an electric mixer they can be whipped up in no time at all. One thing I will advise, though, is that you MUST exercise some patience here and refrigerate them for a good few hours, ideally overnight, to allow them to harden up. This way you can enjoy them at their very best.

2 sticks (1 cup/8oz) unsalted butter (we will be browning this so should end up with 1¾ sticks/7oz)

scant 1 cup (7oz) light soft brown sugar

½ cup (3½oz) superfine sugar

2 teaspoons vanilla bean paste

2 extra-large eggs

1⅔ cups (7oz) all-purpose flour

1 teaspoon fine sea salt

4¼oz white chocolate, broken into small chunks

½ cup (2¼oz) roasted, skinless peanuts, bashed slightly into small chunks

⅓ cup (2½oz) tahini (mix well before using)

2 teaspoons sesame seeds

1. Preheat the oven to 350°F/160°C fan/gas mark 4 and line a deep 8in square cake pan with parchment paper.

2. Melt the butter in a pan over low heat, stirring continuously, for about 10 minutes. You want to take this past the point of melting until it froths vigorously and you start to see light brown solids form at the bottom. Once browned, transfer it to a large bowl to stop it from burning, using a rubber spatula to scrape out all the brown solids, which carry so much flavor. After this process, weigh the butter again (as it loses moisture from the browning process) and top off with regular butter if necessary, so you have 7oz.

3. Add both sugars to the brown butter, and whisk to combine. This can be done by hand—the batter just needs to be homogeneous, not pale and fluffy. Add the vanilla bean paste and whisk again. Make sure the mixture is cool, then whisk in the eggs, one at time, until well combined.

4. In a separate bowl, whisk the flour and salt together. Take out 1 tablespoon and add to a bowl with the chocolate and peanuts and stir to mix. This is to prevent them from sinking. Using a rubber spatula, fold the flour mixture into the wet batter until just combined—don't overmix—then stir in the chocolate and nuts, reserving a handful to sprinkle on top.

5. Pour the batter into the lined pan and drizzle over the tahini in a rough zig-zag pattern, then use a butter knife or skewer and swirl this around. Top with the reserved chocolate and nuts, and finally sprinkle with sesame seeds.

6. Bake in the oven for around 30–40 minutes, until still slightly wobbly in the center, but with firm edges. Allow to cool for 1 hour at room temperature, then transfer to the refrigerator to chill and harden—ideally overnight—or at least 4 hours. Cut into 24 small squares.

TIP

If the peanuts are not already roasted, simply place them in a baking pan and roast in the oven for 10 minutes.

1 Pecan, Coconut, & Caramel Brownies
2 Tahini, Peanut, & White Chocolate Blondies

1

Cakes & Cheesecakes

Mango & Cardamom Cheesecake

I'm not sure whether you'll have tried kulfi before, but it's a traditional, rich ice cream found across India, that's usually flavored with cardamom—and I am obsessed with it. I once had a mango kulfi in Goa, and it was breathtakingly good. So, this cheesecake is a homage to that kulfi—the rich creaminess coming from the cream cheese, paired with sweet mango and floral notes of cardamom. And the cheesecake base is made with spiced speculoos cookies, which complement the cardamom beautifully, in addition to roasted pistachios and coconut for some lovely, nutty flavors and textures. I should also mention that this is a no-bake cheesecake—you may be surprised that something so easy to make can taste so good! There is a long chilling time, so—especially if you're making this for a party—I recommend making it the night before, and then decorating and serving it the next day to wow your guests.

for the base

½ cup (1oz) pistachios
⅓ cup (1oz) shredded coconut
½ stick (2¼oz) unsalted butter (which will be browned so you should end up with 2oz)
1½ tablespoons (¾oz) coconut oil
7oz speculoos cookies

for the cheesecake

10 cardamom pods
¾ cup plus 1 tablespoon (7fl oz) heavy cream, cold
½ cup (2oz) confectioners' sugar
1 teaspoon vanilla bean paste
2⅔ cups (1lb 5oz) cream cheese
2 tablespoons runny honey
scant 1 cup (6½oz) canned, sweetened mango puree

to decorate

1 fresh mango/1 x 15oz (before draining) can of mango
1 tablespoon runny honey
a small handful of pistachios

1. First make the base. Place the pistachios and shredded coconut in a skillet over low heat and toast, stirring, for about 7 minutes until the coconut is golden and nutty. Remove from the heat and set aside.

2. Place the butter in a pan over low heat and stir constantly until you see it bubble up vigorously with a thick, cappuccino-like foam, and then light brown solids will start to form at the bottom. At this point, take the pan off the heat, stirring for about 30 more seconds, then immediately transfer it to another bowl, making sure to scrape out all the solids from the bottom, as these carry so much flavor. Then, stir through the coconut oil until it has melted in the residual heat.

3. Place the speculoos in a sealed freezer bag and bash with a rolling pin until the mixture resembles fine crumbs. Then, add the coconut and pistachios and bash these again to break down the nuts slightly (you can also use a food processor). Tip all the contents into a large bowl and mix with the brown butter and oil until the mixture resembles wet sand.

4. Press this into the base of an 8in springform cake pan, and use the base of a mug to flatten it down. Transfer to the refrigerator to chill and harden while you make the cheesecake filling.

5. Place the cardamom pods in a dry skillet over low heat and toast, stirring, for about 10 minutes until fragrant. Transfer to a pestle and mortar and bash to release the seeds from the shells. Discard the shells (I keep mine and add them to my chai), then grind the seeds into a fine powder. You can also grind the whole pods, including the shells, in a spice grinder.

6. In a large bowl, place the heavy cream, confectioners' sugar, vanilla bean paste and ground cardamom and whisk to fairly stiff peaks.

Continued overleaf >>

7. In a separate bowl, combine the cream cheese, runny honey and ¾ cup (5¼oz) of the mango puree and whisk well to combine. Then, fold through the whipped cream into this cream cheese mixture in three parts, until no streaks remain.

8. Remove the base from the refrigerator and pour half the cheesecake mixture over the top. Then, swirl through half the remaining mango puree and use a knife or skewer to swirl this through the mixture. Then repeat with the remaining cheesecake mixture and mango puree and use an offset spatula to level the top. Place in the refrigerator for 6–8 hours, or ideally overnight, until completely set.

9. To serve, run a frosting spatula or offset spatula around the rim of the cheesecake and then carefully release the springform pan and slide off the metal base.

10. Thinly slice fresh (or canned) mango, and arrange on top of the cheesecake, drizzle over some honey, and sprinkle with pistachios, then slice and serve.

"Mangoes are, hands down, my favorite fruit. When I used to visit my uncle as a child, he would always have a crate full of them—and I would devour so many that I'd end up covered in their sticky, orange goodness!"

Chai Tres Leches Cake

If you haven't had a Tres Leches cake before, you're in for a treat. I had it for the first time in Mexico and I will savor that memory for the rest of my life. Tres Leches is Spanish for "three milks" because there are three (well, in my case, four) types of milk in this recipe—a light, milky, melt-in-your-mouth cake, drenched in a sweet milk mixture and topped with a light whipped cream. And here I am using my favorite drink of all time, Indian Chai, to infuse both the cake AND the milk mixture. We will also be toasting whole spices to really bring out their flavor and infusing the cake and milk mixture with black tea, for that true chai experience.

My mum got me drinking chai. Every chai recipe is different, but of course my bias tells me that my mum's recipe is the best. During lockdown, we sat together and measured out the exact number of cardamom pods and cloves to come up with the perfect balance. This recipe then inspired me to make my first-ever chai-spiced cake, which I made for my *Great British Baking Show* audition, and I then made chai-spiced mini rolls for my first-ever challenge in the tent.

34 green cardamom pods

18 cloves

4½ tablespoons (2¼oz) coconut oil, melted and cooled, plus extra for greasing

6 extra-large eggs, separated

¼ teaspoon cream of tartar (optional)

scant 1 cup (5½oz) superfine sugar, divided in method

½ teaspoon vanilla bean paste

½ teaspoon fine sea salt

1 cup (4½oz) all-purpose flour

½ teaspoon baking powder

2 teaspoons ground cinnamon

2 teaspoons ground ginger powder

for the chai steeping mixture

1⅔ cups (14fl oz) whole milk

4 English breakfast tea bags

¼ teaspoon black pepper

1½ cinnamon sticks

1 teaspoon ground ginger powder

⅔ cup (5fl oz) heavy cream

1 x 14oz can condensed milk

Continued overleaf >>

1. Preheat the oven to 350°F/160°C fan/gas mark 4.

2. First, toast all the spices for the chai steeping milk mixture and the cake together (to save time) and then separate them out. Place the cardamom pods and cloves in a large dry skillet over medium heat and toast them for about 10 minutes until fragrant, then remove from the heat. Separate the cardamom pods from the cloves, then use a spice blender or pestle and mortar to grind the cardamom first, then the cloves separately afterward. (If using a pestle and mortar, then remove the cardamom shells. However, don't chuck these out as they can be added to the steeping milk—as this will be strained—but should not be included in the sponge.)

3. Take out 2 teaspoons of the ground cardamom and ½ teaspoon of the ground cloves and reserve these for the sponge, then place the remaining spices in a large pan for the steeping mixture. To this pan, add the milk, tea bags, black pepper, cinnamon sticks and ground ginger and place over low heat for 10 minutes, stirring every so often. Then take off the heat and set aside to infuse while you make the cake.

4. Grease a large rectangular 8½in x 12in Dutch oven with coconut oil and set aside.

5. Place the egg whites in the bowl of a stand mixer with a whisk attachment (or a large mixing bowl if using a handheld whisk). Add the cream of tartar and beat on a high speed until foamy, then add ⅓ cup (2½oz) sugar slowly, a tablespoon at a time, while still beating on high, until stiff peaks form—be careful not to overwhisk. Transfer to a separate bowl and set aside.

Continued overleaf >>

for the cream topping

3 tablespoons (½oz) shredded coconut
1 cup (8fl oz) heavy cream, cold
1 teaspoon vanilla bean paste
5 tablespoons (2½fl oz) full-fat, canned
  coconut milk, cold
½ teaspoon ground cinnamon,
  to decorate

TIPS

This cake is based on a whisked Genoise sponge, which has more steps than a standard cake, but as long as you follow the recipe carefully, you should have no problems with it. The key is to keep the batter light and airy, so a stand mixer or electric whisk works best. When you add the flour, however, you just want to gently fold it in, to keep the volume in the batter.

Traditional Tres Leches cake uses evaporated milk, but after realizing how hard this is to get hold of, I tried it with whole milk and it works just as well!

6. Add the coconut oil to a small bowl and melt in the microwave for about 45 seconds until smooth. Set aside to cool.

7. Now add the egg yolks to the bowl of the stand mixer (no need to clean out the bowl) and add the remaining sugar with the vanilla bean paste and salt, beating on high until the mixture has doubled in size, is pale yellow and has reached the ribbon stage—meaning that the mixture leaves a trail when you lift the whisk and draw a figure eight.

8. In a separate bowl, place the flour, baking powder, cinnamon, and ginger, and mix together with the reserved, toasted ground cardamom and cloves.

9. Gently fold in half the egg white mixture to the egg yolk mixture until it has mostly been incorporated. Next, sift the flour mixture into this batter in three parts, gently folding each time with a rubber spatula. Then, take about ¼ cup of the batter and mix this with the coconut oil until smooth. Add this mixture back to the batter and fold to combine. Finally, fold in the remaining egg white, until no streaks remain.

10. Pour the cake batter into the greased Dutch oven and tilt it from side to side to level the surface, then bake in the oven for 25–30 minutes, until a skewer comes out clean.

11. Once baked, use a large skewer or fork to poke holes all over the cake, making sure they go all the way to the bottom, then set aside in the dish for about 10 minutes, or until it is cool to the touch.

12. Squeeze the tea bags in the chai steeping mixture, to get as much flavor from them as possible. Then, add in the heavy cream and condensed milk and mix well until combined. Strain the mixture into a pitcher. Pour half of this over the cake, waiting for a few seconds for it to seep in, before pouring over the remainder, leaving about ¾ cup (7fl oz) of the liquid in the pitcher (which will be used to serve with the cake). Cover the dish in plastic wrap and refrigerate for at least 2 hours (or overnight), for the milk mixture to really infuse the cake.

13. When ready to serve, prepare the cream topping. Place the coconut in a large dry skillet and toast, stirring, over low heat for 5–7 minutes, until golden and fragrant. Set aside.

14. In a large (preferably cold) bowl, whisk the heavy cream and vanilla bean paste to almost stiff peaks, then add the cold coconut milk and whisk again until combined and thickened.

15. To assemble, use an offset spatula to spread the coconut cream all over the cake, creating some texture. Sprinkle over the toasted coconut with a light dusting of cinnamon. Cut the cake into squares and serve with some of the reserved chai milk.

Amaretto Coffee Basque Cheesecake

I recently discovered the beauty of Basque cheesecakes, which are nowhere near as daunting as making a regular baked cheesecake because there is no need for a water bath. They are usually flavored with vanilla, but here, coffee, amaretto, and a hint of maple syrup create a mellow, slightly earthy and caramelized flavor profile. And because I want the coffee and amaretto in this recipe to really shine, we will be dividing the cheesecake mix in half and flavoring them both separately, before swirling them together. With individual bursts of coffee and almond flavors running throughout, this couldn't be more delicious.

2 tablespoons instant coffee
  or espresso powder
2 tablespoons hot water
⅓ cup (2½oz) maple syrup
2⅔ cups (1lb 5oz) cream cheese
1 teaspoon fine sea salt
6 tablespoons (2½oz) golden superfine
  sugar
5½ tablespoons (2½oz) light soft
  brown sugar
4 extra-large eggs
⅔ cup (5fl oz) sour cream
scant ½ cup (3½fl oz) heavy cream
1 tablespoon vanilla bean paste
3 tablespoons amaretto
½ teaspoon almond extract
2½ tablespoons (¾oz) all-purpose
  flour

1. Preheat the oven to 520°F/250°C fan/gas mark 10.

2. In a small pan, dissolve the coffee in the hot water and stir in the maple syrup. Place over low heat and stir together for about 4 minutes, until thickened. Once thick, take off the heat, transfer to a bowl and set aside to cool.

3. Using a stand mixer or a large bowl with an electric whisk, mix the cream cheese and salt together with both sugars. Beat for about 3 minutes until smooth.

4. Add the eggs, one at a time, mixing in between each addition and scraping down the sides as needed, until combined. Add the sour cream and heavy cream and whisk lightly until smooth and just combined. Then, sift the flour into the batter, adding it bit by bit and folding until fully combined.

5. Weigh out 9oz of the batter into a separate bowl. To this, add the vanilla bean paste, amaretto, and almond extract and mix well to combine.

6. To the remaining batter, add the cooled coffee-maple syrup mix and whisk to combine.

7. Double line a 8in round cake pan with parchment paper: rotate the second sheet 90 degrees. The paper should be taller than the pan.

8. Pour the coffee batter into the pan first. Then, pour the almond batter over the top in a circular motion, starting from the outside and going in toward the center. Use a frosting spatula to swirl the two batters together and finally lightly tap the pan to remove any air bubbles.

9. Place the pan in the oven and bake for 25–30 minutes, until the top has browned and there is still a wobble in the center—it will continue to cook in the residual heat of the pan.

10. Set aside at room temperature until cool, then refrigerate for at least 1 hour, or overnight, until set. Slice, serve, and enjoy! The cheesecake is great on its own, but I also like it with a small drizzle of maple syrup to complement all the flavors.

TIP

If your oven temperature does not reach 520°F, bake your cheesecake on your oven's maximum temperature, and increase the baking time by a few minutes, until the top is golden with a slight wobble in the middle.

Pistachio, Orange, & Cardamom Carrot Cake

For anyone who watched the *Great British Baking Show* final, this cake will be very familiar. We were tasked with making our own version of a carrot cake for the Signature Challenge, and I came up with this creation. Thankfully, this recipe is easier to assemble than the one I made in the tent - the key is using 10in cake pans: carrot cake is more dense than your standard sponge, so trying to stack a narrow (and taller) cake is tricky (trust me, I learned the hard way!). I also suggest that you make the orange curd first so that it thickens as much as possible before we start assembling (I find 1½ hours is perfect, but you could even make it the night before), otherwise it may be too runny.

for the orange curd (or use store-bought if you're short on time)

6 tablespoons (2½oz) superfine sugar

zest of 3 oranges

juice of ½ orange

2 extra-large eggs

2 teaspoons cornstarch

5 tablespoons (2½oz) cold unsalted butter, cut into cubes

for the carrot cake

1½ tablespoons (¾oz) unsalted butter

1¼ cups (5¼oz) whole pistachios, plus extra to decorate

⅓ cup (1¾oz) walnuts

45 whole cardamom pods

2 cups (9oz) all-purpose flour

2 teaspoons baking soda

½ teaspoon fine sea salt

1½ teaspoons ground cinnamon

1 cup (7oz) superfine sugar

scant 1 cup (7oz) light soft brown sugar

zest of 2 oranges

1¼ cups (10fl oz) olive oil

1 teaspoon vanilla bean paste

4 extra-large eggs

5–6 medium carrots (10½oz), coarsely grated (about 2 cups)

½ cup (2¾oz) raisins

Continued overleaf >>

1. Make the orange curd first as it takes a while to cool down and thicken in the refrigerator. Place the sugar in a small pan along with the orange zest. Mix together with your fingers to release the oils in the zest, which will turn the sugar orange!

2. Squeeze the juice from ½ an orange (which should measure roughly 5 tablespoons/2½fl oz), add to the sugar mixture and whisk to combine, then place this over low heat.

3. In a separate bowl, beat the eggs together, then slowly add the cornstarch, whisking constantly to avoid clumping. Once the orange mixture is hot, slowly pour this over the egg mix in a steady stream, whisking the eggs constantly. Then, tip the whole mixture back into the pan over low heat, switch to a rubber spatula and stir for around 7 minutes until thickened enough to coat the back of a spoon. Take off the heat and whisk in the cold butter cubes until melted, then pass the curd through a mesh strainer and place, covered, in the refrigerator to chill and thicken up for at least 1½ hours, or overnight.

4. Preheat the oven to 350°F/160°C fan/gas mark 4 and line two 10in round cake pans with parchment paper.

5. Melt the butter on a roasting pan in the oven for 5 minutes, then add the pistachios and walnuts to the pan, toss to coat in the butter and bake for 15 minutes until golden. Remove, roughly chop with a knife and set aside.

6. Place all the cardamom pods (yes, 45!) in a large, dry skillet over low heat. Keep stirring for about 10 minutes until fragrant, then transfer to a spice grinder and blitz to a powder, including the pods. If you don't have a spice grinder, you can do this in a pestle and mortar, but it's best to remove most of the shells here if you can't grind them to a fine powder. This should give you 5 teaspoons ground roasted cardamom.

7. In a large bowl, mix together the flour, baking soda, salt, cinnamon, and freshly ground cardamom. In a separate large bowl mix both sugars with the orange zest, rubbing them together with your fingers to release the orange flavor. Then whisk in the olive oil and vanilla paste, followed by the eggs, one at a time, until combined

Continued overleaf >>

Cakes & Cheesecakes

for the frosting

1½ cups (18oz) mascarpone, cold

4 tablespoons runny honey

3 tablespoons vanilla bean paste

6 tablespoons (4¼oz) pistachio cream
(see My Pantry Ingredients on page
10)

⅔ cup (5fl oz) heavy cream, cold

3 tablespoons (¾oz) confectioners'
sugar

TIPS

I'm not being dramatic when I say
that this frosting can be eaten by
the spoonful—it actually tastes
like pistachio gelato. If you have
any left over, freeze it and eat it
like ice cream. It's divine.

However, it does not like the heat
so keep it cold for as long as you
can. And of course, please don't
attempt to frost a warm cake.

8. Fold the dry mixture into the wet mixture in three parts, until
   no flour streaks remain, then add the carrot and raisins, along
   with the toasted pistachios and walnuts and mix to combine.

9. Divide the batter between the lined cake pans and bake in
   the oven for around 35 minutes until a skewer comes out
   clean (note that on different oven racks, each layer may take a
   slightly different time). Once baked, let cool in the tins, before
   transferring to a wire rack and setting aside to cool completely.

10. Now make the frosting. In a large cold bowl, beat the
    mascarpone with the honey, vanilla bean paste and pistachio
    cream until smooth.

11. Separately, in a smaller cold bowl, whisk the heavy cream
    with the confectioners' sugar until it forms stiff peaks—be
    careful not to overwhisk. Fold the whipped cream into the
    mascarpone mix until no streaks remain and place in the
    refrigerator until ready to assemble.

12. Once the cakes are cool to the touch, use a little of the frosting
    to attach the first cake layer to a cake board, making sure
    the flat side of the cake is facing up. Transfer a third of the
    mascarpone frosting to a pastry bag and pipe a circular border
    around the top edge of the cake. Pipe another circle inside
    the first circle, so that they are touching (essentially, you are
    making a double border), and then pipe a final circle on top of
    the two borders.

13. Fill the center with orange curd, leaving about 1 tablespoon for
    decoration.

14. Place the second layer of cake on top, flat side facing down.
    Then, using an offset spatula, spread the top of the cake with
    the remaining frosting (and around the sides too, if you wish).
    Transfer the cake to the refrigerator for the frosting to firm up,
    if needed.

15. Finally, drizzle over the remaining orange curd, decorate with
    more crushed pistachios, then slice and serve.

Mango & Passionfruit Jelly Roll

My favorite fruit in the world is mango and, for me, passionfruit just goes hand in hand with mango. The sweetness from the mangoes with the slightly sharp and fruity notes from passionfruit tastes like a tropical paradise and, here, I've added these flavors to a light jelly roll. We're using canned mango pulp, which is one of my best-loved ingredients to use in baking (more about this in My Pantry Ingredients on page 10). Genoise sponges can be quite tricky to get right (I used to hate making them), but the trick is to whip as much air into the batter as possible, and then to fold the flour in gently to ensure that the air doesn't escape. I recommend a stand mixer for this to achieve a light and airy sponge, or at least an electric whisk.

for the sponge

4 extra-large eggs, separated

¼ teaspoon cream of tartar (optional)

scant ½ cup (3oz) superfine sugar, divided in method

2 teaspoons runny honey

1 teaspoon vanilla bean paste

3 tablespoons (1½oz) canned, sweetened mango puree

1 tablespoon (½oz) coconut oil

¾ cup (3oz) all-purpose flour

½ teaspoon baking powder

¼ teaspoon fine sea salt

a pinch of ground ginger

1¾ cups (7oz) confectioners' sugar, for dusting and rolling

for the passionfruit cream cheese filling

6 passionfruits

⅔ cup (5fl oz) heavy cream, cold

⅓ cup (1½oz) confectioners' sugar

2 tablespoons vanilla bean paste

1 cup (7oz) cream cheese, cold

¼ cup (2oz) canned, sweetened mango puree

1. Preheat the oven to 350°F/160°C fan/gas mark 4 and line a jelly roll pan with parchment paper.

2. Place the egg whites in the bowl of a stand mixer with a whisk attachment (or a large mixing bowl if using a handheld whisk). Add the cream of tartar and beat on a high speed until foamy, then add ¼ cup (1¾oz) sugar slowly, a tablespoon at a time, while still beating on high, until stiff peaks form—be careful not to overwhisk. Transfer to a separate bowl and set aside.

3. Now add the egg yolks to the bowl of the stand mixer (no need to clean out the bowl) and add the remaining sugar with the honey and vanilla bean paste, beating on high until the mixture has doubled in size, is pale yellow and has reached the ribbon stage—meaning that the mixture leaves a trail when you lift the whisk and draw a figure eight. If you're using a handheld mixer, this will take longer than you think, but really ensure that the mixture has grown as undermixing is what can lead to a stodgy sponge. Add in the mango puree and whisk this in to combine.

4. In a small bowl, microwave the coconut oil until it has just melted (about 20 seconds), then set aside to cool.

5. Add half the meringue to the egg yolk mixture and gently fold it in until mostly incorporated. This is to lighten the batter.

6. In a separate bowl, whisk together the flour, baking powder, salt, and ginger, then sift this into the batter in three parts, folding each time with a rubber spatula. Make sure to fold gently so that you do not knock the air out of the batter.

7. Transfer 3 tablespoonfuls of batter to the bowl with the coconut oil and mix to combine, then fold this back into the combined batter. Next, fold the remaining meringue into the entire batter until combined.

8. Fill the lined pan with the cake batter and level out with an offset spatula, taking care not to deflate the batter. Tap the pan gently on the counter to remove any large air bubbles, then bake in the oven for 14–15 minutes, until springy, lightly golden, and a skewer comes out clean.

Continued overleaf >>

Cakes & Cheesecakes

9. Once baked, lay out a sheet of parchment paper on top of a cooling rack and also lay out a clean dish towel, dusted heavily with confectioners' sugar. Flip the sponge onto the parchment paper on the cooling rack, remove the pan and peel off the warm parchment paper. Then, carefully flip the sponge onto the towel, so that the top side is facing up, with the fresh sheet of parchment paper covering it.

10. Using the towel to help you and starting at the short end, slowly roll the sponge up into a log shape. Confectioners' sugar is key here to ensure that the sponge doesn't stick to the towel. Leave the rolled sponge to cool down in a log shape while you make the filling.

11. Spoon the passionfruit pulp into a pan and cook, stirring, over low heat for about 5 minutes until thickened, then set aside to cool completely.

12. Next, combine the heavy cream, confectioners' sugar and vanilla in a large bowl and whip into almost stiff peaks, making sure not to overwhisk.

13. Place the cream cheese in a bowl and beat this to loosen, then add the cooled passionfruit pulp and mix to combine. Next, fold in the whipped cream in three parts and, finally, swirl through the mango puree, leaving large streaks in the mixture.

14. To assemble, carefully unroll the cake, making sure not to rip the sponge, and remove the parchment paper. Spread the filling all over with a frosting spatula. Carefully reroll the sponge, then wrap the whole jelly roll tightly with plastic wrap, twisting the ends to form a sausage (this will help to retain the shape). Transfer to the refrigerator to chill for an hour.

15. To serve, remove the plastic wrap and then dust the roll with confectioners' sugar. Or, if you have leftover frosting, you can pipe or spread this on the outside of the sponge too. Slice and serve.

TIP

I never discard passionfruit seeds because it's wasteful, and I love the crunch that they add too.

Lime, Coconut, & Sesame Cake

This is my take on the classic lemon loaf cake, except that I've changed almost every single ingredient... but with good reason! There's something about lime, versus the standard lemon, that just provides an extra fresh and sharp flavor. Here, it's balanced out with the nutty and rich flavors of coconut and sesame.

for the sponge
½ cup (1¾oz) shredded coconut, plus extra to decorate

3 tablespoons black sesame seeds, plus extra to decorate

3½ tablespoons (1¾oz) unsalted butter, at room temperature

generous 1 cup (8oz) superfine sugar

zest of 3 limes, plus extra to decorate

1½ tablespoons (¾oz) coconut oil, melted

½ teaspoon vanilla extract

¼ teaspoon coconut extract (optional)

3 eggs

scant ½ cup (3½fl oz) coconut cream, room temperature

1⅓ cups (5½oz) all-purpose flour

1½ teaspoons baking powder

¼ teaspoon fine sea salt

for the lime frosting
scant 1 cup (3½oz) confectioners' sugar

juice of 2 limes

TIP

The black sesame seeds add a lovely visual element to the cake (think of it as a step up from poppy seeds) but if you can't get your hands on black ones, white will do—you just won't have that speckled crumb.

1. Preheat the oven to 350°F/160°C fan/gas mark 4 and line a 8½in x 4½in x 2½in loaf pan with parchment paper.

2. Place the shredded coconut and sesame seeds in a dry skillet and toast over low heat for about 5–7 minutes until golden. Transfer to a bowl and set aside.

3. Beat the butter in a bowl until soft and creamy (a stand mixer works best here to beat in enough air). In a separate bowl, combine the sugar and lime zest and use your fingers to rub these together, which will release the oils from the zest and create a lovely citrus aroma, and turn the sugar green! Then, add the zesty sugar mix to the butter, and beat this together until combined, scraping down with a rubber spatula every so often.

4. Add the coconut oil and beat until pale and fluffy (for about 7 minutes on a stand mixer), then add the vanilla bean paste (and coconut extract, if using) and beat again. Add the eggs, one at a time, mixing until fully incorporated before adding the next.

5. Melt the coconut cream in the microwave for 10–15 seconds until smooth but not hot.

6. In a separate bowl, sift in the flour, baking powder and salt and whisk to combine. Then, using a rubber spatula, fold the dry mix into the batter in three parts until no streaks remain, alternating with the coconut cream—be careful not to overmix. Finally, add the toasted coconut and sesame seeds, reserving some of the garnish, and fold this into the batter until well dispersed.

7. Pour the batter into the lined loaf pan, level out with a rubber spatula, then bake in the oven for around 50 minutes, until a skewer comes out clean. Allow to cool in the pan before transferring to a wire rack.

8. While the cake is cooling, make the lime frosting. Place the confectioners' sugar in a bowl and add the lime juice, bit by bit, until it forms a thick but runny consistency.

9. Once the cake is cool, use a spoon to drizzle the frosting all over the top, then sprinkle over the reserved shredded coconut, sesame seeds and lime zest. Leave this to stand for about 10 minutes, to allow the frosting to firm up slightly, then slice and serve!

"My first memory of sesame as a child was in the form of those sesame brittle bars, and I'd always get bits stuck in my teeth. They were sweet, crunchy, and nutty—and I could go through about five packages in a day."

Fig & Rose Mascarpone Cheesecake Bars

Okay, I know that rose water can be off-putting, because it can taste like an old lady's bathroom, or a bowl of potpourri. However, if you get the balance right, with just a hint of rose, it can really bring your desserts to life. Here, I've paired it with sweet and spicy stem ginger, honey, and crunchy pistachios, all enveloped in creamy mascarpone with caramelized roasted figs. It is the perfect dessert for a dinner party and isn't sickly sweet, thanks to the mascarpone, which leaves you wanting more and more!

for the roasted figs

10 small figs (12oz), cut into eighths
1 tablespoon melted unsalted butter
1 tablespoon honey
1 teaspoon stem ginger syrup

for the base

1¾ cup (3½oz) pistachios
5¼oz gingersnaps
¾ stick (3oz) unsalted butter

for the cheesecake

generous 1 cup (14oz) mascarpone,
    at room temperature
6 tablespoons (3oz) honey, plus
    2 tablespoons to garnish
3 tablespoons stem ginger syrup
1 teaspoon vanilla bean paste
3 teaspoons rose water
1 teaspoon ground ginger powder
¼ teaspoon fine sea salt
1¼ cups (10fl oz) heavy cream
3 bulbs stem ginger (2¼oz),
    finely diced (1 tablespoon)
½ teaspoon rose petals, to decorate

1. Preheat the oven to 400°F/180°C fan/gas mark 6.

2. First prepare the figs. Arrange the fig slices in a shallow baking sheet lined with parchment paper. Mix together the melted butter, honey, and stem ginger syrup, then pour over the figs, tossing them gently to ensure that they are coated in the glaze.

3. Place in the oven and bake for 15 minutes, until sticky and soft, then set aside to cool.

4. Meanwhile, roast the pistachios on a baking sheet for 10 minutes, until slightly golden and fragrant.

5. Place the gingersnaps in a food processor and then blitz to the size of large crumbs. Add the roasted pistachios (reserving 1 tablespoon for decoration) and pulse again until broken down slightly. Transfer these to a large bowl.

6. Melt the butter in a pan (or microwave), then add this to the crumbs and mix until the mixture resembles wet sand.

7. Take a deep, rectangular baking dish (28 x 18 x 1in) lined with parchment paper and tip the cookie mixture into the dish. Using an offset spatula or the bottom of a jar, flatten down the mixture until it is nicely compact and there are no gaps. Place this in the refrigerator to chill and harden while you make the mascarpone filling.

8. In a large bowl, whisk together the mascarpone, honey, stem ginger syrup, vanilla bean paste, rose water, ground ginger and salt until combined.

9. Place the heavy cream in a separate bowl and whisk until almost stiff peaks, making sure not to overwhisk. Then, fold this into the mascarpone mixture in three parts.

10. Add the stem ginger to the mixture, along with the roasted figs (saving a few for decoration), along with any roasting juices and fold these in.

11. Remove the chilled base from the refrigerator and pour the filling on top. Level this out with an offset spatula or frosting spatula, then press the remaining figs down on top of the filling. Place the cheesecake back in the refrigerator to set for a minimum of 4 hours, or overnight.

12. Before serving, drizzle over honey and sprinkle with rose petals and the reserved pistachios, chopped. Cut into 16 slices.

9

Desserts, Tarts, & Puddings

Rasmalai-inspired Bread & Butter Pudding

Growing up in a Goan household in the UK and with a sweet tooth, there were always two desserts that would light up my face at a family gathering: bread and butter pudding, and rasmalai. They are extremely different in nature and flavor—bread and butter pudding is a comforting, warm British classic, with a slight custardy feel to it, whereas rasmalai is a cold milky dessert, flavored with cardamom and saffron (and just tastes utterly divine). So, naturally, I decided to combine both desserts together, which means that I no longer have to choose between the two! We have ingredients from a classic bread and butter pudding, but infused with all the flavors and textures from rasmalai—it's one of my favorite desserts in this book!

¾ cup (1½oz) pistachios

scant ½ cup (1¾oz) whole almonds, skin on

15 cardamom pods

1⅔ cups (14fl oz) whole milk

¾ cup plus 1 tablespoon (7fl oz) heavy cream

scant ½ cup (2¾oz) superfine sugar

a big pinch of saffron

10 slices brioche bread

4 tablespoons (2¼oz) unsalted butter, softened, at room temperature

3 extra-large eggs

⅓ cup (1¾oz) golden raisins

2 tablespoons turbinado sugar

1. Preheat the oven to 350°F/160°C fan/gas mark 4.

2. Roast the pistachios and almonds in a roasting pan in the oven for 15 minutes, until slightly golden and toasted. Allow to cool slightly before roughly chopping with a knife into small chunky pieces (we want these to add crunch).

3. Place the cardamom pods in a dry skillet over medium heat and toast for about 10 minutes, stirring constantly, until slightly golden and fragrant. Transfer to a pestle and mortar (or spice grinder), bash them to remove the seeds (reserve the shells), and grind these into a fine powder.

4. In a medium pan, place the milk, cream, sugar, saffron, and ground cardamom, along with the shells, and mix to combine. Heat gently for 10 minutes, stirring constantly, then turn off the heat and let infuse while you prepare the bread. (Once infused, remove the cardamom shells.)

5. Spread each slice of brioche with butter, then cut each slice into nine small squares and set aside.

6. Crack the eggs into a large bowl and whisk to combine. Then, carefully pour in the milk mixture, bit by bit, whisking constantly until combined.

7. In a 5-quart square Dutch oven, sprinkle over half the brioche pieces to cover the bottom. Sprinkle over half of the roasted nuts and golden raisins, then pour over half the custard.

8. Repeat this process with the remaining ingredients and, finally, sprinkle turbinado sugar on top. Let soak for 10 minutes, then bake in the oven for around 25 minutes, until slightly golden and crunchy on top, and soft and custardy underneath.

9. Serve this on its own or with a scoop of pistachio ice cream on the side, which is my personal favorite!

"Cardamom is my favorite spice by a country mile. For me, it's linked to so many family recipes from my Goan heritage. As soon as I start toasting those cardamom pods, the familiar, warming smell fills my kitchen with so many memories."

Lime, Kiwi, & Coconut Eton Mess

During my time on *The Great British Baking Show*, I created a "Kiwi Lime Pie" pavlova. It went down a treat, and I've been dying to make it again. However, to remove the stress of making a whole pavlova, I found that this works perfectly as an Eton Mess, which is what I present to you here. There are many "stars of the show." First up, the simple addition of toasted coconut to the meringue makes them somewhat reminiscent of coconut macaroons, and they are utterly divine. My tangy lime curd has a lower sugar content than most recipes, to ensure that it balances with the sweet meringue, and the finishing touch of coconut whipped cream and fresh kiwis turns this into a fresh, light, flavor-packed dessert, with little surprises in every bite.

for the meringue

1 cup (3½oz) shredded coconut
1 teaspoon white wine vinegar
4 egg whites (4½oz)
¼ teaspoon cream of tartar
1¼ cups (9oz) superfine sugar
½ teaspoon vanilla bean paste

for the lime curd

zest and juice of 6 limes
¾ cup (5¼oz) superfine sugar
4 extra-large eggs
1 teaspoon cornstarch
generous 1¼ sticks (5½oz) cold
    unsalted butter, cut into cubes

for the whipped cream

1 cup (8fl oz) heavy cream, cold
5 tablespoons (2½fl oz) coconut
    cream, cold
1 teaspoon vanilla bean paste
½ cup (1¾oz) shredded coconut

to decorate

10 kiwis, diced
zest and juice of 2 limes
coconut flakes

TIP

This recipe makes a few extra meringues, but you will be snacking on them for a while. Store in an airtight container for up to 2 weeks.

1. First make the meringue. Preheat the oven to 250°F/100°C fan/gas mark ½. In a large skillet over a low heat, toast all of desiccated coconut (150g) for the meringue and the cream, stirring for 5–7 minutes until golden and fragrant. Remove from the heat and set aside to cool.

2. Wipe down a large mixing bowl with a little vinegar to make sure it is clean and dry. Place the egg whites in the bowl with the cream of tartar and use an electric whisk on medium speed until you reach the soft peak stage.

3. Lower the speed, add in the sugar, a couple of tablespoons at a time and ensure that it has all dissolved before adding the next. Scrape down the sides of the bowl with a clean rubber spatula as needed to ensure that all the sugar is incorporated.

4. Once all the sugar has been added, increase the speed and whisk the mixture until it is thick and glossy, and holds stiff peaks. Rub a small amount of the meringue mix between your fingers—continue whisking if it feels grainy. Once the meringue is ready, add the vanilla and whisk again, then fold in ½ cup (3½oz) of the shredded coconut, reserving the rest for later.

5. Transfer the meringue to a pastry bag and cut off the tip to form a small hole, about ¾in diameter.

6. Pipe meringue kisses on two large baking sheets lined with parchment paper. Transfer to the oven and then bake for 1 hour 15 minutes. Turn off the oven and leave the door ajar (propped open with a wooden spoon) for 15 minutes. You can leave the meringue kisses to cool in the oven for as long as the rest of the dessert takes to make, and then remove once ready to assemble. Once completely baked, they should easily peel off the parchment paper.

Continued over leaf >>

7. As soon as the meringues are in the oven, start making the lime curd. Place the lime zest and sugar in a heavy pan and use your hands to mix them together to release the oils—turning the sugar a pale green color. Then, squeeze the juice of the limes directly into the pan with the zest and sugar. Lightly beat the eggs and pour these into the pan along with the cornstarch, mixing well to combine.

8. Place the pan over low heat, whisking regularly to ensure that all the ingredients are homogeneous, then switch to a rubber spatula and continue mixing until the curd has thickened—it should be thick enough to coat the back of the rubber spatula.

9. Once the curd has thickened, take the pan off the heat and whisk in the cold butter until it has melted. Pass the lime curd through a fine mesh strainer into a clean bowl and discard the remnants in the strainer. Cover the bowl with plastic wrap and place in the refrigerator to allow it to cool completely.

10. Now make the whipped cream. Place the cream in a cold metal bowl and whisk to medium peaks—do not overwhisk. Add the coconut cream and vanilla bean paste, and whisk until almost stiff peaks. Finally, fold through the remaining shredded coconut. Keep this in the refrigerator until ready to assemble.

11. Before assembling, place the diced kiwi in a bowl, pour the lime juice on top and mix to combine.

12. Lightly crush the meringues and place one in the bottom of 10 tall serving glasses. Top each crushed meringue with 2 tablespoons of lime curd, followed by 2 tablespoons of coconut cream, followed by a sprinkle of diced kiwi. Repeat these layers until you reach the top of each glass.

13. Decorate with a sprinkle of the lime zest and coconut flakes if you wish, then enjoy.

Malted Milk Chocolate & Hazelnut Mousse Pie

This no-bake creation is definitely a nod to my childhood and those malted milk cookies that I adored! And, of course, those malty flavors go perfectly with chocolate, as do hazelnuts, which provide a lovely texture. The chocolate mousse here could not be simpler to make as it involves no eggs. I've included a quick extra step to keep the base nice and crunchy, by painting it with a layer of chocolate, sprinkled in hazelnuts—so don't skip this step. My lactose-intolerant uncle ate a huge slice of this and loved it, so I hope that shows you how much my family are obsessed with this one!

for the shell
scant 1 cup (4oz) hazelnuts
scant 1 stick (½ cup/3¾oz) unsalted butter (this will be browned, so we should end up with 3½oz)
10oz malted milk cookies
1½oz milk chocolate

for the mousse
2 cups plus 1 tablespoon (17fl oz) heavy cream
1 tablespoon vanilla bean paste
⅔ cup (2½oz) chocolate malt powder
9oz good-quality milk chocolate, roughly chopped
½ teaspoon fine sea salt

for the cream topping
½ cup (4fl oz) heavy cream
1½ tablespoons chocolate malt powder

to garnish
¾oz milk chocolate
¼ cup (¾oz) malted milk cookies, crushed

TIP
If you can't get your hands on malted chocolate powder, use either regular drinking malt powder or failing that, regular unsweetened cocoa powder (though the malt flavor will not be strong).

1. Preheat the oven to 350°F/160°C fan/gas mark 4.

2. First make the shell. Place the hazelnuts in a baking pan and roast for 10 minutes until lightly golden and fragrant, then transfer to a bowl and set aside to cool. Weigh out 2 tablespoons (¾oz), roughly chop them and reserve for decoration.

3. Melt the butter in a large pan over low heat for about 10 minutes, stirring continuously, until browned. You want to take it past the point of melting until it froths vigorously and you start to see light brown solids form at the bottom. Immediately take it off the heat, stirring continuously for a few more seconds, then transfer to a large bowl to stop it from burning and use a rubber spatula to scrape out all the brown solids, which carry so much flavor.

4. Place ½ cup (2½oz) of the hazelnuts with the cookies in a food processor (or a sealed freezer bag), and blitz or bash to a sandlike consistency. Add this to the brown butter and mix until well incorporated and the mixture resembles wet sand.

5. Tip your cookie mixture into the bottom of a loose-bottom 9in fluted tart pan. Use a rubber spatula to flatten it down and your fingers to push the mixture into the ridges of the tart pan and up the sides. Once smooth, place this in the refrigerator for 30 minutes to chill and harden.

6. Melt 1½oz milk chocolate in the microwave in 20 second bursts, then use a brush to paint the inside of the cookie base all over with chocolate. Break up ¼ cup (1oz) of the hazelnuts into small chunky pieces and sprinkle these on top of the chocolate, then return the base to the refrigerator to set, while you make the chocolate mousse.

7. In a large pan combine half the heavy cream with the vanilla bean paste and scant ½ cup (1¾oz) of the chocolate malt powder and mix until combined. Place this over low heat and stir for a few minutes until steaming, but not boiling.

Continued overleaf >>

8. Place the milk chocolate in a large heatproof bowl and, once the cream mixture is hot, pour this on top. Let stand for 30 seconds, then slowly mix with a rubber spatula, starting from the middle, until the chocolate has melted and mixed well with the cream, with no streaks remaining.

9. Transfer the ganache to the refrigerator to chill until cool to the touch, but still soft. Once the ganache is cool, you can prepare the cream.

10. Place the remaining heavy cream in a large bowl with the salt and remaining 3 tablespoons (¾oz) chocolate malt powder and whisk with an electric whisk until you have medium peaks. Fold this cream into the ganache in three stages, until no streaks remain.

11. Remove the cooled tart shell from the refrigerator and pour in the mousse.

12. Return it to the refrigerator to set for 2 hours, or overnight.

13. Once set, remove the tart from the pan. To do this, slide a small frosting spatula underneath the tart pan, in between the bottom of the tart pan and the fluted rim. Run the knife all around the bottom as the melted butter may have stuck this together. The tart should then pop out easily.

14. Before serving, prepare the topping. In a large bowl, whip the cold heavy cream with the chocolate malt powder until it forms medium peaks. Using a frosting spatula, spread this on top of the set mousse, forming some peaks in the cream. Finally, using a grater or a sharp knife, create large shavings of milk chocolate and sprinkle these all over the cream, along with the crushed cookies and reserved hazelnuts. Slice and enjoy!

TIPS

Don't use a perforated pan when making a no-bake crust, because everything will seep through! I've also included some tips in the method for when it comes to unmolding the tart shell, as it can be tricky with no-bake crusts.

Heavy cream whips best when cold, so keep this cold until ready to use.

Miso Caramel, Apple, & Pecan Galette

What I love about galettes is that they're a very informal pastry. They're free-form, rough around the edges and the shape is a bit different every time, but that gives them their charm. In my recipe, miso caramel sauce is what really elevates this humble galette—the miso offsets the sweetness of the caramel, which makes it dangerously moreish. For me, the best way to enjoy this is to pour the sauce all over your pastry, and not hold back. I promise, it won't be sickly sweet.

for the pastry

¼ cup (1oz) pecans
2 cups (9oz) all-purpose flour
scant ½ cup (3oz) superfine sugar
1 teaspoon ground cinnamon
½ teaspoon fine sea salt
10½ tablespoons (5½ oz) unsalted butter, cold/frozen, cut into cubes
2¼oz egg yolk (approximately 3 yolks), whites reserved
turbinado sugar, for sprinkling

for the miso caramel sauce

⅔ cup (5fl oz) heavy cream
1½ tablespoons white miso paste
scant 1 cup (6¾oz) light soft brown sugar
2½oz white chocolate, chopped into small pieces

for the filling

1 cup (4¼oz) pecans
3 medium Granny Smith apples, peeled and thinly sliced
2 tablespoons all-purpose flour
½ cup (4½oz) miso caramel sauce (see above)
1 teaspoon white miso paste

TIP

The pie dough has ground pecans and a hint of cinnamon, which pairs really well with the apples and pecans. However, if you're short on time, you can of course use store-bought pastry.

1. Preheat the oven to 350°F/160°C fan/gas mark 4.

2. Place all the pecans needed for the pastry and filling (10½ tablespoons/5½ oz) in a large baking pan and roast in the oven for 15 minutes, until toasted and fragrant. Remove ¼ cup and pulse in a food processor to a fine powder and set this aside for the pastry. Pulse the remaining 1 cup into small pieces, but not too fine, as we want some texture. Set aside.

3. Now make the pastry. In a food processor (or large bowl), place the flour, sugar, cinnamon, salt, and the powdered pecans and pulse or mix to combine. Add the cold butter and pulse until broken down slightly, but remaining chunky (the size of a walnut). Use your hands if you don't have a food processor. Whisk the egg yolks and slowly add this to the mixture, pulsing or mixing until it forms a dough. Add a few tablespoons of ice-cold water if needed. As soon as the mixture forms a dough, stop mixing, as overworking this dough will make it tough.

4. Remove the dough from the bowl, press down slightly, then wrap in plastic wrap and chill in the refrigerator for 30 minutes.

5. While the dough is chilling, make the miso caramel sauce. Pour the cream into a pan, whisk in the miso paste and place over low heat until steaming but not boiling. In a separate, deep pan put the sugar and ¼ cup (2fl oz) water and stir over low heat until the sugar has dissolved. Once dissolved, bring this to a boil without stirring.

6. Pour the cream slowly into the sugar mixture, stirring constantly, then place back over low heat and cook for a few minutes until bubbling or reaches 221°F/105°C on a sugar thermometer.

7. Place the white chocolate in a heatproof bowl and pour the caramel over the chocolate. Leave it to stand for a minute, then stir slowly with a rubber spatula until the chocolate has melted and combined with the caramel. Place the caramel sauce in the refrigerator to cool and thicken, stirring occasionally.

Continued overleaf >>

8. To make the filling, put the apple slices in a large bowl, sprinkle over the flour and mix well with your hands to ensure that all the slices are coated. Measure out the ½ cup of the caramel sauce and whisk in the additional miso paste until combined. Pour this over the apples and mix until they are thoroughly coated.

9. Roll the pastry out on either a floured silicone mat or a piece of parchment paper (this will make it much easier to transfer to the baking sheet) and shape into a 13in-diameter circle. In the middle (to make approximately a 9in diameter circle) brush over 2 tablespoons of the caramel sauce. Sprinkle the chopped pecans over the caramel, reserving 2 tablespoons for decoration.

10. Arrange the apple slices in a layer over the pecans, starting from the outside and working in a circular fashion, with each slice overlapping the other slightly. Repeat this with more layers of apples until they are used up. Carefully fold the pastry over the edge of the apples, making about six large folds so it looks roughly like a hexagon.

11. Use the reserved egg white to brush over the pastry border, and then sprinkle over the turbinado sugar. Chill the galette in the refrigerator for 30 minutes, or the freezer for 15 minutes.

12. Preheat the oven to 375°F/170°C fan/gas mark 5 and place a large baking sheet inside to heat up.

13. Carefully transfer the pastry, with the parchment paper or silicone mat underneath, to the hot baking sheet in the oven and bake for 50–55 minutes, until the pastry is golden, puffed up slightly, and the apples are cooked all the way through.

14. Sprinkle the galette with the reserved pecans and drizzle over some of the caramel sauce. Serve with more sauce on the side and a scoop of ice cream.

Spiced Ginger Sticky Toffee Pudding

In the world of sticky desserts, my favorites are sticky toffee pudding and Jamaican ginger cake—so of course I had to combine the two! The result is something quite splendid—comforting, familiar, but with a warming spice and a hint of rum to make this feel slightly more grown up. The addition of black tea provides a lovely earthy backdrop to the sweet dates, with spiced rum, stem ginger and its syrup to really accentuate those spicy flavors, and brown butter in the sticky toffee sauce to add a lovely, nutty undertone. This is perfect for a dinner party, or a great way to end a Sunday roast.

for the sponge

1 black tea bag
1 cup (5oz) roughly chopped soft dried pitted medjool dates
1 teaspoon baking soda
5½ tablespoons (2¾oz) unsalted butter, room temperature, plus extra for greasing
3½ tablespoons (1¾oz) dark muscovado sugar
2 tablespoons corn syrup
1 tablespoon stem ginger syrup
2 extra-large eggs, at room temperature
1⅓ cups (5½oz) all-purpose flour
2 teaspoons baking powder
½ teaspoon fine sea salt
6 teaspoons ground ginger powder
1 teaspoon ground nutmeg
1 teaspoon ground cinnamon
3 tablespoons spiced rum
4–5 stem ginger bulbs (3½oz), finely diced (2 tablespoons)

for the sauce

10½ tablespoons (5½oz) unsalted butter, softened
⅔ cup (5½oz) dark muscovado sugar
scant ½ cup (3½oz) light soft brown sugar
¾ cup plus 1 tablespoon (7fl oz) heavy cream, plus extra to serve
3 tablespoons stem ginger syrup
2 teaspoons ground ginger powder
¼ teaspoon fine sea salt
2 tablespoons spiced rum

1. Preheat the oven to 350°F/160°C fan/gas mark 4.

2. Place the tea bag in a medium bowl, and pour over ¾ cup (7fl oz) boiling water. Press the tea bag slightly to help it infuse the water, then add the dates and baking soda. Mix well to combine. Set aside to soak while you make the batter.

3. In the bowl of a stand mixer (or a large bowl), beat the softened butter with the sugar until fluffy (this may take around 7 minutes, depending on the power of your mixer). Add the two syrups and beat again to combine. Add the eggs, one at a time, making sure to mix the first in well before adding the second, and scraping down the sides with a rubber spatula as needed.

4. In a separate bowl, combine the flour, baking powder, salt, ground ginger, nutmeg, and cinnamon and whisk well to combine. Fold this into the wet batter in three parts, until no flour pockets remain.

5. Transfer the soaked dates, along with the liquid, to a food processor and blend with the spiced rum until almost smooth (a few lumps are fine). Add this mixture to the batter along with the stem ginger and fold until combined.

6. Grease a 9in square baking dish with butter and pour in the batter, flattening out the top with a frosting spatula. Bake for 25–30 minutes, until a skewer comes out clean.

7. While the sponge is baking, make the sauce. Melt the butter in a large pan over low heat, stirring continuously. You want to take it past the point of melting until it froths vigorously and you start to see light brown solids form at the bottom, which takes about 10 minutes. At this point, take it off the heat, continuing to stir, add the two sugars and mix well to combine. Add the heavy cream, stem ginger syrup, ground ginger and salt and mix again.

8. Return the pan to the heat for a few minutes, until the sauce is bubbling and slightly thickened. Add the spiced rum, mix to combine, then take off the heat.

9. With a skewer or fork, prick the baked sponge all over, then pour a quarter of the sauce on top. Set aside to soak for 30 minutes. Slice and serve with a generous drizzle of the remaining sticky toffee sauce and more cream, if you like.

Tahini, Dulce de Leche, & Chocolate Chip Ice Cream

Firstly, no ice-cream maker is needed for this recipe, so it couldn't be easier! Now, as for the flavor... well, as you know, I am quite obsessed with tahini in sweet foods and this, paired with the sweet caramel notes from the dulce de leche, is a match made in heaven. The ice cream also has lots of texture, with toasted sesame seeds and finely chopped chocolate chips to really bring it to life. This isn't the sort of ice cream that you serve to accompany a dessert—this IS the dessert. It really needs its own spotlight.

1 x 14oz can condensed milk (or ready-made dulce de leche)

1 tablespoon (½oz) white sesame seeds

1 tablespoon (½oz) black sesame seeds

2½oz semisweet chocolate

1¾oz milk chocolate

4 tablespoons (2¼oz) tahini, at room temperature

2½ cups (20fl oz) heavy cream, cold

½ teaspoon fine sea salt

1 tablespoon vanilla bean paste

TIPS

I use a potato peeler to get the semisweet chocolate really fine. The texture I aim for is like that in stracciatella, or mint choc chip ice cream.

If you don't have a microwave, melt the chocolate in a bowl placed over a pan of hot water, making sure the water does not touch the bottom of the bowl.

1. First, make the dulce de leche (if not using ready-made dulce de leche). Remove the labels from the unopened can of condensed milk and completely submerge it in a large pan filled with water. Cover tightly with a lid and boil for at least 4 hours—you want a really strong color on your dulce de leche. Check the pan every so often to ensure the water is not evaporating and top off if necessary. After 4 hours, switch off the heat and use tongs to carefully remove the can from the water, and allow it to cool before using. If you boil it for a shorter amount of time, the dulce de leche will be lighter, and the flavor of your ice cream base will not be as strong.

2. Place the white and black sesame seeds in a dry skillet and toast over low heat for around 5 minutes until fragrant. Remove from the heat and set aside.

3. Using a potato peeler, shave the semisweet chocolate very finely and set aside.

4. Place the milk chocolate in a bowl and melt in the microwave in 20-second bursts. Once the chocolate has melted, mix in the tahini. It is important that your tahini is at room temperature, as otherwise the mixture could seize. Set this aside.

5. In a large bowl, combine the heavy cream, salt, and vanilla bean paste and then whip using an electric whisk until soft peaks form.

6. Transfer your dulce de leche to a separate bowl. It will be quite solid, so stir it until loosened. Add the dulce de leche to the cream in three parts, whisking between each part until smooth.

7. Add the sesame seeds and chocolate shavings (reserving a tablespoon of each for decoration) and fold these into the mixture until well dispersed.

8. Pour half of the ice cream into a loaf pan, then pour over half the chocolate-tahini mixture, and swirl this with a knife or a skewer. Repeat with the remaining ice cream and chocolate tahini mixture. Finally, top with the reserved sesame seeds and chocolate shavings, and place in the freezer for 5 hours or overnight. Allow the ice cream to soften at room temperature slightly before serving.

Yuzu & White Chocolate Mousse

If you're a fan of anything citrus, you will LOVE yuzu. The flavor is very strong, so I like to pair it with something sweet, to balance out the sharpness, which is why it works so perfectly in this white chocolate mousse. It's light, delicate, and airy, but has such a beautifully balanced flavor running throughout. And the best part is that this is made using just five ingredients!

4 extra-large eggs
⅔ cup (4½oz) superfine sugar
¼ teaspoon fine sea salt
6 tablespoons (3fl oz) yuzu juice
2¾oz white chocolate, chopped, plus extra to decorate

1. First make the yuzu curd. Crack two eggs into a bowl. Separate the remaining two eggs, reserving the whites and add the yolks to the bowl, along with ⅓ cup (2½oz) of the sugar and the salt. Whisk to combine.

2. In a pan, gently heat the yuzu juice with ¼ cup (1¾oz) of the sugar, until it almost reaches a simmer. Slowly pour this yuzu mixture into the egg mixture, whisking constantly, until combined.

3. Return the mixture to the pan and place over low heat, mixing with a rubber spatula, for 5–7 minutes, until it starts to thicken. Don't be tempted to turn up the heat as it can curdle—slow and steady is key here. You want it thick enough to coat the back of the spatula.

4. Place the white chocolate in a bowl, then strain the curd through a fine mesh strainer, directly onto the chocolate. Stir gently with a rubber spatula until the chocolate has melted into the mixture, then set aside to cool at room temperature. Once cool, cover with plastic wrap and place in the refrigerator for 1 hour, or until completely cool.

5. Once the curd is cool to the touch, place the reserved egg whites in a large bowl (or stand mixer) and whisk with an electric whisk until very foamy. Gradually add the remaining 2 tablespoons of sugar, whisking constantly, until the mixture forms almost stiff peaks, then use a rubber spatula to gently fold the egg whites into the curd, in three parts, until no white streaks remain.

6. Pour the mousse into six serving glasses or ramekins and refrigerate for at least 30 minutes before serving.

7. To serve, use a sharp knife to carefully shave very thin slices of white chocolate then sprinkle them over the top.

TIP

Sadly, I have not come across a fresh yuzu in my lifetime, but luckily there are some fantastic good-quality bottled yuzu juices out there (see My Pantry Ingredients on page 10), which I use in this recipe.

Gingerbread Latte Custard Pie

Warming, spicy, and sweet, with a hint of coffee—a gingerbread latte is my favorite thing to drink at Christmas; it's like a festive hug. Here, I've taken its essence and transformed it into a custard tart. We've got a sweet pie dough shell with ground pecans and ginger for extra flavor. The custard is infused with all the warming spices (which are toasted, to maximize their flavor), with brown sugar for some delicious caramel notes. And the tart is finally topped with a light whipped cream, infused with a hint of coffee, to really complete the latte flavor. And don't worry—this definitely isn't reserved just for Christmas!

for the custard

4 cloves
4 teaspoons ground ginger powder
1 teaspoon ground cinnamon
generous ¾ cup (7fl oz) whole milk
1¼ cups (10fl oz) heavy cream
1 tablespoon vanilla bean paste
1 strip of orange zest
½oz fresh ginger, cut into thick strips
8 egg yolks
3½ tablespoons (1¾oz) dark soft brown sugar
3½ tablespoons (1¾oz) light soft brown sugar

for the pastry

2 cups (9oz) all-purpose flour
¼ cup (1oz) ground pecans
scant ½ cup (3oz) superfine sugar
¼ teaspoon ground ginger powder
½ teaspoon fine sea salt
generous 1¼ sticks (5½oz) cold unsalted butter, cut into cubes
2¾oz egg yolks (3 egg yolks), whites reserved

for the cream topping

scant ½ cup (3½fl oz) heavy cream, cold
1 teaspoon vanilla bean paste
2 tablespoons (½oz) confectioners' sugar
½ teaspoon espresso powder
2 teaspoons honey
ground cinnamon, for dusting

1. First up is the custard. To ensure that this has as much flavor as possible, it's important to infuse the milk for as long as we can. Place the cloves, ground ginger and cinnamon in a large dry pan over low heat and stir for about 10 minutes until fragrant.

2. Pour in the milk and cream, along with the vanilla bean paste, orange zest and fresh ginger and heat gently for 15 minutes, stirring every couple of minutes. Then, take this off the heat and set aside to infuse for as long as you want (even overnight). If you plan to make the dessert the same day, leave this to infuse in the pan while you make the pastry.

3. Preheat the oven to 350°F/160°C fan/gas mark 4 and place a baking sheet on the bottom rack.

4. Now, make the pastry. In a food processor (or a large bowl), place the flour, ground pecans, sugar, ground ginger and salt. Pulse or mix to combine. Add in the cold butter and pulse or use your hands until the mix resembles bread crumbs. Gradually add the egg yolks and pulse or combine until it forms a dough. Add a few tablespoons of ice-cold water if needed. Make sure not to overmix the dough as it can become tough.

5. Remove the dough from the bowl, press down slightly, wrap tightly in cling film, then place in the freezer for 15 minutes to chill and firm up slightly.

6. Once chilled, remove the plastic wrap and place the pastry on a lightly floured counter or silicone mat. Using a floured rolling pin, roll it out into a large circle ⅛in thick, using a 9in tart pan as a guide. Roll the pastry up on the rolling pin, place at the top edge of the pan, and roll out over the pan. Working quickly, press the pastry down into the corners. Leave any excess pastry to hang over the edge as this will be trimmed later. Prick the pastry all over with a fork, then put it back in the freezer for 6 minutes to harden.

7. Scrunch up a piece of parchment paper, then flatten it out and place it inside the pastry shell, then fill this with pie weights, or uncooked rice. (Scrunching it up first helps it to fit more neatly inside the pastry).

Continued overleaf >>

8. Remove the hot pan from the oven, place the tart on top, then return it to the oven and blind-bake for 15 minutes.

9. After 15 minutes, take out the parchment paper and pie weights and carefully trim off any overhanging pastry.

10. Brush the reserved egg white in a thin layer over the bottom of the pastry, then place the tart back in the oven for another 15 minutes.

11. Once baked, take the tart out of the oven and set aside, then turn the temperature down to 275°F/120°C fan/gas mark 1.

12. Now, it's time to finish the custard. Place the infused milk back over low heat. In a large bowl, whisk together the egg yolks with the two sugars until combined. Then, slowly whisking (we don't want too many bubbles) gradually pour the hot, infused milk over the egg yolk mixture. Remove the cloves, orange peel and fresh ginger, then transfer the custard to a pitcher and skim off any foam from the top.

13. Place the tart shell on the large baking sheet in the oven, and slowly pour the custard into the pastry, holding the pitcher as close to the pastry as possible, again to avoid too many bubbles. If any do form, skim them off with a spoon (this will ensure that the custard is silky and smooth at the top), then bake in the oven for 40 minutes, until firm with a slight wobble in the center. Remove and allow to cool then transfer to the refrigerator to cool completely while you make the cream topping.

14. In a large bowl, combine the heavy cream, vanilla bean paste, confectioners' sugar, espresso powder and honey and whip to medium-stiff peaks.

15. Ensure the custard tart is cool to the touch, then spread the coffee cream all over the custard and, finally, sprinkle with a small dusting of cinnamon (which is how I like to top my lattes). Slice and serve!

TIP

If you're short on time, you can use store-bought pie dough, but just note that this won't have the added flavor of ginger and pecans.

Tahini, Coffee, & Date Rice Pudding

Little cans of rice pudding filled me with so much joy as a child. So, I've taken one of my favorite childhood desserts and made it slightly more grown up—paired with earthy coffee, nutty notes of tahini and sweet dates. When I was making this for the first time, I only had soya milk in the house, but it actually worked perfectly in the recipe thanks to its slight nutty flavor. And, by the way, the coffee flavor isn't very strong as I found that just 2 teaspoons are enough to add a lovely mellow backdrop, which tastes more like a latte (versus a strong espresso).

⅓ cup (2¼oz) pudding rice or long grain rice

2 tablespoons unsalted butter

1½ tablespoon (¾oz) soft dark brown sugar

2¾ cups (22fl oz) unsweetened soya milk

2 teaspoons instant coffee

¼ cup (1½oz) finely chopped pitted medjool dates

½ teaspoon fine sea salt

4 tablespoons white sesame seeds per serving, to decorate

¼ cup (2fl oz) heavy cream, plus extra for drizzling

3 tablespoons tahini

for the date caramel

⅔ cup (4½oz) pitted medjool dates

⅔ cup (5fl oz) hot water

½ teaspoon vanilla bean paste

2 tablespoons heavy cream

TIPS

This will thicken as it cools so, if you are not eating it immediately, I recommend adding a good splash (another 1fl oz or so) of soya milk before serving and stirring it through.

To make this vegan, use vegan butter instead of regular butter, and swap the heavy cream for coconut cream (or a vegan cream alternative).

1. Wash and drain the rice in cold water a few times until the water runs clear. Set aside.

2. Melt the butter in a large pan over low heat, stirring continuously until it begins to brown and smell nutty. Tip in the washed rice and stir for a couple of minutes until all the rice is coated in the butter. Add the sugar and stir again until well coated.

3. Add 2⅔ cups (21fl oz) of the soya milk, along with the coffee, chopped dates and salt and stir well to combine. Turn the heat down as low as it can go and be patient—we want to cook this really low and slow because, if the liquid evaporates too quickly, the rice won't cook through.

4. Cook the rice pudding for at least an hour (possibly 15 minutes longer), stirring every now and again to avoid the rice sticking at the bottom. Don't worry if the milk looks like it's splitting at the beginning—this will be the dates breaking down in the milk and, as the mixture thickens, the milk will turn creamy and homogeneous.

5. While the rice pudding is cooking, make the date caramel. In a bowl, put the dates in the hot water to soften for about 10 minutes. Once soaked, transfer the dates and the soaking water, along with the vanilla bean paste and cream to a blender and blitz until smooth. Set aside.

6. Toast the sesame seeds in a dry skillet over low heat for about 7 minutes until nutty and slightly golden. Set aside.

7. When the rice pudding is cooked through and creamy, turn off the heat, cover with a lid, and allow to steam for 15 minutes. This will ensure that every grain is cooked. After this time, stir through the remaining 2 tablespoons (1fl oz) soya milk along with the heavy cream and tahini and mix well to combine.

8. Divide the rice pudding between serving bowls, top with a good drizzle of the date caramel, plus a little extra cream and a generous sprinkle of toasted sesame seeds. Serve immediately.

Index

Conversion Charts

WEIGHT

5 g	⅛ oz		175 g	6 oz		700 g	1 lb 9 oz
10 g	¼ oz		200 g	7 oz		750 g	1 lb 10 oz
15 g	½ oz		225 g	8 oz		800 g	1 lb 12 oz
25/30g	1 oz		250 g	9 oz		850 g	1 lb 14 oz
35 g	1¼ oz		275 g	9¾ oz		900 g	2 lb
40 g	1½ oz		280 g	10 oz		950 g	2 lb 2 oz
50 g	1¾ oz		300 g	10½ oz		1 kg	2 lb 4 oz
55 g	2 oz		325 g	11½ oz		1.25 kg	2 lb 12 oz
60 g	2¼ oz		350 g	12 oz		1.3 kg	3 lb
70 g	2½ oz		375 g	13 oz		1.5 kg	3 lb 5 oz
85 g	3 oz		400 g	14 oz		1.6 kg	3 lb 8 oz
90 g	3¼ oz		425 g	15 oz		1.8 kg	4 lb
100 g	3½ oz		450 g	1 lb		2 kg	4 lb 8 oz
115 g	4 oz		500 g	1 lb 2 oz		2.25 kg	5 lb
125 g	4½ oz		550 g	1 lb 4 oz		2.5 kg	5 lb 8 oz
140 g	5 oz		600 g	1 lb 5 oz		2.7 kg	6 lb
150 g	5½ oz		650 g	1 lb 7 oz		3 kg	6 lb 8 oz

VOLUME

1.25 ml	¼ tsp		150 ml	5 fl oz / ¼ p		700 ml	1¼ pint
2.5 ml	½ tsp		175 ml	6 fl oz		850 ml	1½ pint
5 ml	1 tsp		200 ml	7 fl oz / ⅓ p		1 litre	1¾ pint
10 ml	2 tsp		225 ml	8 fl oz		1.2 litres	2 pints
15 ml	1 tbsp / 3 tsp / ½ fl oz		250 ml	9 fl oz		1.3 litres	2¼ pints
30 ml	2 tbsp / 1 fl oz		300 ml	10 fl oz / ½ pt		1.4 litres	2½ pints
45 ml	3 tbsp		350 ml	12 fl oz		1.7 litres	3 pints
50 ml	2 fl oz		400 ml	14 fl oz		2 litres	3½ pints
60 ml	4 tbsp		425 ml	15 fl oz / ¾ pt		2.5 litres	4½ pints
75 ml	5 tbsp / 2½ fl oz		450 ml	16 fl oz		2.8 litres	5 pints
90 ml	6 tbsp		500 ml	18 fl oz		3 litres	5¼ pints
100 ml	3½ fl oz		568 ml	1 pint			
125 ml	4 fl oz		600 ml	20 fl oz			

Thanks

Thank you to God and to many angels up above who have helped me get here. A special mention to my late Grandad Gregory, who I had the privilege of living and growing up with, and who always knew I had a passion for food—we used to watch cooking shows together, and he even called me "Masterchef" (touchy I know, given the *Great British Baking Show* rivalry and all that). I wish he was here to see me with a published cookbook in my hands.

Thank you to my irreplaceable family, especially mum, dad, my sisters, Chanelle and Corelle, and my brother-in-law Vignan. They have, more than anything, had to deal with the disgraceful mess in the kitchen while I have been cooking and baking away, splattering oil all over the stovetop, spilling confectioners' sugar on the floor, or splashing buttercream on the ceiling (don't ask). Thank you for your love and your prayers. Thank you for encouraging me to apply for *The Great British Baking Show*, even though I was convinced I wasn't good enough, and for supporting me every step of the way throughout my career. You've been with me through the highest and lowest parts of my life and I wouldn't be here today without you.

Mum, a special thanks to you for instilling a love of food in me, for teaching me the foundations of flavor, and for your honest (sometimes brutal) feedback, which has helped me so much throughout my recipe testing.

Dad, thank you for the sacrifices you made throughout your life, to give my sisters and I a good education, and one that you never had. Your hard work and desire to chase your dreams is what inspires me every day to do the same.

Auntie Hazel—thank you for being my inspiration, and the main reason why I started baking in the first place. Your selflessness and willingness to help me throughout my baking journey has been invaluable and I will be forever grateful. Nana Julie, thank you for your love, prayers, and support throughout the years.

I didn't realize just how much goes into a book, and so for that, I have an army of people to thank, who made this book happen. Thank you to Jo, Izzy, Yasia, and the whole team at Kyle Books for believing in me and my vision with this book, for being so patient with me and my crazy ideas, and for giving me the chance to share my passion for flavors with the world.

Thank you to Vanessa and her wonderful assistant Carl, who brought my vision to life, photographing every dish so beautifully, as well as David who shot the front cover. You were all a sheer joy to work with.

Thank you to my incredible food stylists, Katie and Esther, and their assistants, Caitlin and Maria who worked tirelessly on the shoots, often in the sweltering heat! The Beyoncé playlists coupled with your fantastic energy made every shoot day an absolute blast.

Thank you to everyone from Love Productions and *The Great British Baking Show* who believed in me, and gave me the best start to a dream career in food.

Thank you to my agents, Alex, Milly, and Stan, for your continued support and guidance with my new career.

And, finally, I want to thank YOU—my readers. Thank you for picking up a copy of *Flavor Kitchen* and choosing to cook from my recipes. Your kindness, positivity, and support have helped me turn my passion into a career, and I am so very grateful.

Crystelle

www.crystellepereira.com | Instagram: @crystellepereira
TikTok: crystellepereira | Facebook: @crytellepereiraofficial

An Hachette UK Company
www.hachette.co.uk

First published in Great Britain in 2023 by Kyle Books,
an imprint of Octopus Publishing Group Limited
www.kylebooks.co.uk

ISBN: 978 1 91423 979 3

Text copyright © Crystelle Pereira, 2023
Design and layout copyright © Octopus Publishing Group Ltd, 2023
Photography copyright © Vanessa Lewis, 2023
Cover photography © David Reiss 2023

Distributed in the US by Hachette Book Group,
1290 Avenue of the Americas,
4th and 5th Floors, New York, NY 10104

Distributed in Canada by Canadian Manda Group,
664 Annette St., Toronto, Ontario, Canada M6S 2C8

Crystelle Pereira is hereby identified as the author
of this work in accordance with Section 77 of the
Copyright, Designs, and Patents Act 1988.

Publisher: Joanna Copestick
Editor: Isabel Jessop
Art Director: Yasia Williams
Copy-editor: Vicki Murrel.
Photographer: Vanessa Lewis
Food stylists: Esther Clark & Katie Marshall
Production Controllers: Lucy Carter & Nic Jones

Printed and bound in China.

10 9 8 7 6 5 4 3 2 1